HOPING IN SOLITUDE

Antonio Fernando Ramón René Gerardo

Editorial Capitán San Luis
Havana, 2008

Text translation: Juanita F. Vera
Poetry translation: Julio Llopi, Ana Portela, Ana Elena Garazoza
Cover design: Based on the oil painting by Ernesto M. Rancaño,...where men are born...
Cover design: Eugenio Sagués
Interior design: Rafael Morante
Text digitalization: Zoe Cesar
Computer design: Norma Ramírez Vega
Original title in spanish: Desde la soledad y la esperanza

All rights reserved
© On the present edition.
2008, Editorial Capitán San Luis

ISBN: 978-959-211-317-6

Imprime: ESCANDÓN IMPRESORES. Sevilla

Editorial Capitán San Luis, Ave.25 no.3406, entre 34 y 36, Playa
La Habana, Cuba

Partial or complete reproduction of this book, including the cover, or its transmission in any way or by any means is totally forbidden without prior authorization of this publishing house.

HOPING IN SOLITUDE

Why am I innocent?
Because no country should punish another people's children for
the same reasons that would make heroes of its own.

RENÉ GONZÁLEZ SEHWERERT

roberto fernández retamar

Prologue

This book comes as a full complement of another one edited by the same publishing house under the title *Scars in the Memory*. Both deal with the same subject, i.e. terrorism, and they do it with a similar perspective. But while the previous book touched on some of the many attacks the Cuban people has been, and still is, the direct or indirect target of, due to the mischievous actions of successive US Administrations through almost half a century, the present volume focuses on five young Cubans. These men risked their lives to monitor the counterrevolutionary groups based in Florida. They were bent on preventing new actions against our country, and eventually against others. This is then a book about five anti-terrorist Cubans who have saved a countless number of lives, — not only Cuban lives — which they preserved with their tenacious work. Upon learning of such work, the US authorities, which fathered those groups and continues to protect them, had these anti-terrorists incarcerated in very hard conditions, submitted to a judicial farce in the city of Miami, and condemned to unlikely sentences. As for Cuba, its National Assembly of People's Power, following a suggestion from comrade Fidel, unanimously agreed to grant them the official title of Heroes of the Republic of Cuba.

It is indispensable that first and foremost the American people but, in general, good-willing men and women all over the world become acquainted with the case of these five Cuban heroes who have been put behind bars in that country's prisons for fighting terrorism while the leaders of that country have unleashed a monstrous endless war allegedly to fight terrorism.

The extraordinary Court statements of these five men, included in this volume, offer an unequalled possibility to appreciate their mettle. These statements were first presented on the eve of the announcement of the ominous rulings against them, but an updated assessment of their situation has also been included in this book. It is also worthwhile taking note of some of the compelling works created by these men in the strenuous conditions imposed on them, for these men who withstand a most unfair treatment are not only brave, which they have proven to be, but also talented, and that gift has endured despite efforts to suffocate it. From their bleak and desolate prisons they bring to light moving and incisive productions where their noble spirits shine.

For the Cuban people these five men are five more sources of pride. There is not one single genuine compatriot who does not want to help them some way, to give one piece of their own to those that gallantly and selflessly spared us more grief. As for the present book, writers, visual artists and musicians residents in this country have joined to offer their works, above all to help in spreading as extensively as possible the truth about the scandalous case of the Cuban Five. Interpreting some words by Mario Benedetti that I already mentioned in the prologue to the other book, these are urgent works. There is no doubt that some of them will survive the present circumstances, but they have all been born from these specific circumstances with the intent to be useful. In the homeland of José Martí this intent or the usefulness of art under certain conditions, will not come as a surprise, albeit there is much valuable art created with other purposes.

It is with a justified combination of modesty and pride that writers and artists with a recognized work are showing here their commitment to one of the noblest duties we have today, that is, to contribute to spreading the truth about the monstrous injustice committed against five men who not only enhance the country where they were born but also humanity at large. When the truth is fully known, the certainty bursting from deep in our hearts will become a reality, and they will be back!

Havana, April 19, 2007
"Year 49th of the Revolution"

Because, in the end, we shall rest free and
victorious beneath that sun which we are
denied today.

ANTONIO

eduardo heras león

To Tony, Mirta and Maruchi

WRITING À LA CARTE

He had just got home, mentally exhausted as usual, and this time even somewhat dizzy after climbing the stairs. He thought it was due to the degenerative osteoarthritis in his neck diagnosed only a few days before. The flickering light of the answering machine drew his attention and following the daily routine he pressed the button to listen to the messages. A voice he could not identify said that it needed to talk to him for an urgent work, to please call back, and it left a number. He decided to rest for a while, to heat up a bit of coffee and to savor it leaning back with half-closed eyes while listening for the umpteenth time, at full volume, Verdi's *Nabucco* choir, which always had the same soothing effect on him.

The coffee relaxed him, so he pressed the *repeat* button of the answering machine to listen to the message again. This time he took note of the telephone number and decided to respond the call. The voice on the other side sounded familiar.

—I'm glad you're calling because I was about to call you again.

—What's that urgent work you have, José Ramón? Now everybody seems to be in a hurry wanting things right away. What's up with you? He said sounding upset.

—I'd rather explain it personally, the other said shyly.

—No, no, you tell me now, What's up? Wait, I'll turn down the music. He pushed the *clear* button on his remote control and the music went off. OK, go on…

—It's a contribution for a book we're planning to produce.
—Ah! A contribution. I assume you want me to edit the book, right?
—No, the idea is that you write a text; fiction, if possible.
—But, I'm so busy! You must be mad. I'm fully engaged. I have no spare time.
—It doesn't have to be a long text, and we really need your contribution. It's indispensable. We have already talked with a group of authors and they are very excited about the idea.
—That's good, man, but it's impossible for me; I really can't. I really can't do it.
—Look, wait, you don't need to respond now. Sleep on it and I'll call you back.
—I'm sorry, brother, but I can't.
—Hey, man, it's an important book.
—So, it is. And, what's the subject?
—It's about the five heroes imprisoned in the United States.
—My God! I don't do that!
—Why not?
—Because it's the same old story, José Ramón, literature à la carte. I always shy at that because I'm no good at it. I've tried it before, and it doesn't work. I can't do it; I simply don't know how to do it.
—Wait, wait, we'll talk about it later. I'll be sending some materials on them that I have here; you read them and then you tell me. Look, even if you don't do anything. I know how you feel about this kind of literature. I'm only asking you to read the material. We'll talk later. Then he made a long pause.
—OK, then; I'll read them but you already have my answer.

José Ramón had hung the phone, but he still heard the dial tone for a few more minutes. He didn't want to say why he couldn't take any other work. He was trying to complete the editing of a novel; he had just signed the contract and he would be paid good money for it. He would do that work against all odds. The repair of the bathroom, an old dream that did not materialize and that was postponed one month after the other, depended on that money that he would receive in a few days. The situation was unbearable, with all the pipes closed down, the leaking through the roof and the humidity spoiling the walls. That bathroom was going to cost him a divorce: "At least, I want to see you start fixing it, to show that you care for this house," his wife had said, almost furious. So, now everything else could wait. The bathroom had to be new when she returned from her trip to Venezuela. This was his number-one priority and he would not miss the chance due to a last minute nuisance.

He went back to bed, pressed the button in the remote control and listened to the deep chords of the *Nabucco*; that choir seemed to convey all the sadness in the world and it always had the effect of bringing tears to his eyes. He thought he was becoming more sentimental, but listening to that music was one of his ways to combat stress. According to the doctor, aesthetic emotion was good to bring relief to both body and soul. José Ramón was always coming up with new projects and it was true he had contributed before but this time it was different. He was being asked something he couldn't do, even if he wanted to; even if he were willing to put aside the novel knowing he would have a memorable discussion with his wife. Writing *à la carte* meant going against everything he believed in about literature, against everything he had learned after so many years in this trade. Literature had to flow spontaneously from deep inside, from emotions, from an esthetic training, from dreams and imagination. He agreed with Cortazar that writing was an action beyond will, like a medium engaged by a foreign force. That was also the way he wrote, and he couldn't think of doing it any differently.

He walked to the window in the living room and opened it. A hot breeze covered his face and he felt like a warm mist was caressing him. He went to the sound system and looked up among a pile of CDs until he found Rachmaninov's Concerto No.2, his favorite. He wanted to go on feeling that, partly excited by the music because he wanted to catch up speed to finish the edition of that novel, which he had promised himself to complete in a couple of days. He took a quick look at the bathroom and the sound of the leaking pipes started to get on his nerves. He closed the door and went back to bed.

He recalled that at some point he had tried to write differently, so he had stuffed himself with old essays by Sartre on that issue of intellectual commitment, when the writers divided into practically two groups: those committed to society and their times, and those committed only to their own work. And even if in theory he had defended his admired Sartre, in practice it had been impossible to follow those ideas that he found so attractive. However, at the other end of the road he didn't find an answer either. In the 1960s, language became fashionable as a protagonist of works. Down with the content; the argument does not exist. The story is bullshit. Form is essential. But, what about exploitation and poverty, and struggle and the revolution? Who writes about that? What can a writer do faced with such reality? Can he overlook it? Can he pitifully turn his head and go on writing *the* Work? God, had this dilemma been discussed here, too! And it had been costly!

He smiled thinking that he had a dilemma now: paradoxically, his decaying bathroom was *the* work and José Ramon's work was reality. And he would not hesitate here. What else could he do? When faced with that dilemma years ago, he had always avoided a concrete response. Yes, he had been an opportunistic at times. Before certain officials he had advocated the writer's and the work's commitment to reality while before other writers he had defended the opposite. Lately, Saramago had said something very lucid: that he took on his commitment to his work as a citizen and a man of his times; but he was also committed to his work, which didn't have to be measured with the same yardstick.

The work was the work without interference from anyone but its own creator. That seemed to him the ideal position, so he had made it his own. And now, the same old story hit home. Anyway…no material would make him change his position. The bathroom was also his work…and he fell asleep.

Early the following day he was awaken by the doorbell. Half asleep and staggering he opened the door and through the railings somebody handed him an envelope.
—From the Publishing House.
'José Ramón doesn't give up," he thought and smiled.
After having breakfast, shaving and taking a shower he decided to take a look at the content of the envelope. Actually, he had the day open, for in addition to giving the final touches to the revised novel, he was planning to write a couple of pages for Cubarte, the WEB site dedicated to culture, and he estimated that two or three hours would suffice to write a chronicle on the chess match he had had with Che in the now distant 1960s that he had never been able to take off his memory.

He opened the envelope and went through its content: magazines, pictures, speeches, graphic material on the Five Heroes and their Court statements. He had a first reaction to put everything aside, but then he thought he had promised Jose Ramón to read the material so he chose to do it. He didn't know much about the case or rather he had some idea from what he had seen on television, the daily propaganda on the case, and Fidel's and Alarcon's speeches on the issue. And, of course, he was sympathetic with their struggle; as a citizen of this country he was in solidarity with the campaign for their return. He had once heard Mirta, the mother of Tony Guerrero whose poems he had read, and he was moved by her words, by the extraordinary serenity that she exuded, by that aura of sadness but also of energy that illuminated her eyes, as if suddenly grief and despair for the separation from her son and for his incarceration were replaced by confidence in his return. And he couldn't help it; he had walked up to her and kissed her cheek.

He didn't know much about the others, either. But he had read interviews with their wives and children, and the life of each of those men had struck him as an excellent material for various novels, because in every one of them there were beautiful love stories.

Then he started reading. He became acquainted with details on the case: their arrests on September 12, 1998, the prison, the violation of legal procedures, the rulings, the prison terms, and the silence of the media. It all seemed an unheard-of conspiracy. But, above all, he realized that the sentences made a mockery of justice. He decided to read last their Court statements. These were impassioned and moving oratory pieces. Ramón had said at the end of his statement: "I will wear the prison uniform with the same honor and pride with which a soldier wears his most prized insignia!" And Fernando had said: "Throughout the years of my imprisonment, I will always carry with me the dignity I have learned from my people and their history." René did not ask for clemency for him, but for "justice for my comrades, accused of crimes they did not commit," and Gerardo concluded with the words of the American patriot Nathan Hale: "My only regret is that I have but one life to give for my country." Then it fell on him that those were more than simple phrases. They had been said by men who were challenging an injustice, a destiny that would inevitably be adverse on them, and against which there was nothing they could do. They had to be sincere phrases, even if they sounded commonplace.

He took a break. The telephone had been ringing and immersed in his reading of the materials he had not paid attention. He felt overwhelmed and nothing better than a strong coffee to clear his head and proceed with the reading. He went to the kitchen like a robot, set up the coffee maker and a few minutes later he gulped down a cup of sugarless coffee, and went back to the materials.

He took another quick look at what he had read and noticed he had one last Court statement, Tony Guerrero's. Almost intuitively he had left it for the end, since in addition to his poems, particularly the sonnet "I'll be back", which now again he had before his eyes and whose final verses read: "I shall sing my songs to destiny/ and my voice will make death quiver," always moved him deeply.

Still under the strong impression of the sonnet, he read the Court statement: it was a long poem, which under Whitman's composition and through the voices of Martí, Maceo and Mario Benedetti demanded "only justice, for the wellbeing of our peoples, for the wellbeing of truth," and concluded with some prophetic words: "Because, in the end, we shall rest free and victorious beneath that sun which we are denied today." He had been through practically all of the material and when he was to return them to the envelope he realized there was still one testimony he had not read, it was from Tony, written five years after those sentences. He made a quick reading but then stopped in a paragraph that read: "I remember that December 27, while returning to the area where I was secluded, an inmate of Cuban descent came up to me; he knew the sentence already […] so he asked me how I felt. I didn't stop to think if he was moved by good or bad intentions, I didn't care; I honestly and shortly answered him: "It's the happiest day of my life."

He couldn't go on reading. How is this possible? He said to himself. How could it be the happiest day of his life? He finished putting all of the materials back in the envelope but then he came across a picture of Tony Guerrero and he stopped for a few minutes to look at it. This was an ordinary man like any other you pass by in the streets, but he was staring back from the picture in a way he wanted to describe but couldn't, and so he started searching his memories, the many readings he had made in his life, and in that search in his mind he found an old fisherman, a sturdy and implacable man fighting the forces of nature symbolized in an enormous marlin fish, and Hemingway's phrase to describe him, gave him the key to the picture: "and his eyes were joyful and unbeaten."

And then he wanted to promise himself something, and he took Tony's photo as a witness. He promised that he would write that text or at least he would try. It would take him some time. He had never done something like that and he was not sure of the result, if at the end it would be something good or just correct. He stood up and went to the bathroom. Possibly the repair would have to wait a little longer. The next time his wife called he would explain the reasons, and perhaps she would understand, perhaps not…

The concerto was advancing towards the final majestic chords and he decided to call José Ramón. He picked up the phone but before he dialed any number he felt an irrepressible impulse. He went to the computer, turned it on and when it was ready he sat down and started to write: "He had just got home…"

April 2007

Free as a bird   Eduardo M. Abela

Defense statement presented by Antonio Guerrero Rodríguez at the sentencing hearing held on wednesday, december 27, 2001

*Now on this spot I stand with
my robust soul.
Walt Whitman
(From Song of Myself)*

Your Honor,

Allow me to say that I share everything that has been said in this courtroom by my four brothers in arms: Gerardo Hernández, Ramón Labaniño, René González and Fernando González. They spoke with dignity and courage to the Court. Our speeches are based on the strictest truth, on the soundness of the principles we embrace and in the honor of the heroic Cuban people. It is only fair to say that the lawyers and their assistants acted in a highly professional, honest and courageous manner and that the translators, Liza, Richard and the marshals worked in a very ethical and professional way.

At the beginning I wrote in my diary of my long days, "... a real man does not look to see on which side one lives best, but on which side lies duty". Those are José Martí's words, which a century after they were written still encourage, live and are the essence of what is most pure and altruistic.

It is often difficult
To find the exact words,
But these have been in me
Beaten
Shaken

Incubated by the truth,
Waiting to break the shell and see the light.
And the day has come.
Allow me to explain my reasons, your Honor, in the clearest and most concise way:

Cuba,
My little country, has been
Attacked,
Assaulted,
And slandered
Decade after decade
By a cruel
Inhuman and absurd
Policy.

A real terrorist war,
Fierce and open,
The harbinger of horror
Of sabotage,
A ruin, murder maker
A grief carrier,
Of the most profound grief,
Death.

This aggression has been exposed not only by documents and information from the Cuban government but also by secret documents that the very government of the United States has declassified.
This aggression has included the CIA's recruiting, financing and training counter-revolutionary agents; the Bay of Pigs Invasion; Operation Mongoose; pretexts for military intervention; plans to assassinate heads of State and Government; infiltrations by armed groups; sabotage; violations of our airspace; spy flights, spraying with bacteriological and chemical agents; machine gun fire on our coasts and buildings; bombs in hotels and other social, cultural, historic and tourist centers, all kinds of cruel and vicious acts of provocation.

And the outcome of these acts:

More than three thousand four hundred dead; more than two thousand people left totally or partially handicapped; substantial damage to the economy, the source of our livelihood; hundreds of thousands of Cubans who are born and grow up under a harsh blockade and in a hostile cold war climate. Terror, hardships and pain have been brought over the entire population.

Where have such unceasing ruthless acts been hatched and financed?

For the most part, in the United States of America.

What has the government of this country done to avoid them?

Practically nothing.... And the aggression has not ceased...

Today, people who are responsible for some of these actions still walk freely the streets of Miami. And radio stations and other media give coverage to and instigate new acts of aggression against the Cuban people.

Why so much hatred for the Cuban people?
Is it because Cuba chose a different road?
Because its people want socialism?
Because it did away with the large estates
and wiped out illiteracy?
Because it gave free education
and medical care to its people?
Because it lets
the dawn break freely over its children?

Cuba has never placed the security of the United States in jeopardy nor committed any act of aggression or terrorism against it. It deeply loves peace and quiet and wants the best relations between our two countries. It has shown that it admires and respects the American people.

"Cuba is not a military threat to the United States," Admiral Carroll said in this courtroom.

General Atkinson testified that Cuba presents "zero" military threat to the United States.

It is my country's unquestionable right –like that of any other— to defend itself against those who try to harm its people.

The job of putting a stop to these terrorist acts has been complex and difficult because the terrorists have enjoyed the complicity or lax tolerance of the authorities.

My country has done everything possible to warn the US government of the danger of these acts and to do so it has used official, unofficial and public channels. However, such cooperation has never been reciprocated.

In the nineties, fired up by the demise of the socialist camp, terrorist groups intensified their activities against Cuba. It was, they felt, the long dreamed hour for stirring up the final chaos, for terrorizing the people, destabilizing the economy, damaging the tourist industry, building up a crisis and dealing the death blow to the Cuban Revolution.

What could Cuba do to defend itself and be forewarned of the terrorist plans against it? What could it do to avoid a greater conflict? What options did it have to safeguard its sovereignty and the safety of its children?

One way to prevent these brutal and bloody acts, to prevent the suffering becoming worse because of more deaths was to move quietly.

There was no alternative but to rely on men who –out of love for a just cause, out of love for their country and their people, out of love for peace and life– were prepared to voluntarily agree to carry out this honorable duty against terrorism, that is, to give advanced warning of the danger of attack.

The reason behind my acts and the motive for doing my duty, the same as my comrades', has been to prevent a conflict that would bring sorrow to our peoples.

We were not moved to do what we did by money or resentment. It did not occur to any of us to harm the noble and hard-working American people. We did nothing detrimental to the national security of the United States. The court records show it. Those who doubt my words may examine them and find the truth.

The barbaric attacks on the World Trade Center and the Pentagon last September 11 filled with indignation everyone who loves a peaceful world. The unexpected and unwonted deaths of thousand of this country's innocent citizens pierced our hearts with deep sorrow.

Nobody can deny that terrorism is an inhuman, ruthless and repugnant phenomenon that must be eliminated with the utmost urgency.

"And in order to make sure that we're able to conduct a winning victory, we've got to have the best intelligence we can possibly have." "Unity is needed to strengthen the intelligence agencies, so that we can learn what the plans are before they are implemented and to discover the terrorists before they attack."

These two statements were not made by the president of the Republic of Cuba, our Commander in Chief Fidel Castro, but by the president of the United States, after these horrendous attacks. I have wondered over and over again. Are these statements not valid for Cuba, which is a victim of terrorism?

This is exactly what Cuba has done to try to put an end to this scourge, which has also buffeted her territory for so many years and made martyrs of her people. Your Honor,
A "trial" took place
This courtroom knows as much,
We lived together and we lived through days full of statements
Testimony,

Circumstantial evidence,
Evidence,
Arguments,
Motions,
Commitments,
Doubts,
Slanderous allegations,
Falsehoods,
Deliberations,
I didn't come here today to justify anything,
I came to tell
The truth:
"That is the only thing I am committed to."

Accord; there was none except the commitment to be useful to the world, to serve a valid cause called humanity and also motherland.

Intent, there was none except to prevent senselessness and crime and to save the living flower from chance, sudden, pointless and premature death.

There was no transgression and no offense. Nobody was insulted.

Nothing was stolen. No one was deceived. No one was cheated.

No one tried to or practiced espionage.

Nobody ever asked me to get any classified information. Here in this courtroom the witnesses' statements confirmed that, not only defense witnesses but also those of the prosecution itself.

Read General Clapper's, Joseph Santos' and General Atkinson's testimony, to name but a few, and they will confirm what I say in all honesty.

And many other people could have come to this court to explain things about my life, to say what I did every day just as Dalila Borrego, Edward Donohue, and Tim Carey came. On the other hand, nobody came here to speak against me, nor would it be possible to find anyone who, in all sincerity, could point to any failing in my conduct in this society.

I love the island where I grew up, where I was educated and where my mother, one of my beloved children, many of the people I love and many of my other friends live. I also love this country where I was born, where, over the last ten years, I have given and received real proof of love and solidarity.

I am certain that a bridge of friendship will definitely be laid not only between these two peoples but also among all the peoples in the world.

It falls to you, your Honor, to hand down sentence in this long and tortuous trial. Bring proof and evidence together!

Voices will say that they don't exist.
Take into account facts and arguments!
Voices will say they carry no weight:
Read cases and testimony!
Voices will say it is not possible
To blame these men.
Voices that arise from the heart itself.
Voices inspired by the strength of justice.
Voices which did not want to be, or which were not
Listened to by a jury
Which could not serve justice.

They were wrong! Their verdict was sacrilege. But we were aware, from the beginning, that when it comes to Cuba, Miami is an impossible place for justice.

This has been, above all else, a political trial.

Personally, I ask for nothing else but justice; for the good of our countries, for the sake of truth. A fair, full sentence, free from political strings, would have sent an important message in this crucial moment in the fight against terrorism.

Allow me to repeat that I have never caused personal harm to anyone not have caused any property damage. I have never tried to take any action, which would endanger the national security of the United States.

If I were asked to do the same thing again, I would do it with honor. An excerpt from a letter that Cuban general Antonio Maceo, who fought for Cuban independence in the 19th century, wrote to a Spanish general comes to mind at this time with force and passion:

"I shall not find any reasons for having cut myself off from humanity. I pursue not a policy of hatred but of love; this is not an exclusionist policy but one founded in human morality".

Because of your rulings, my beloved brothers and I must be unjustly kept in prison, but there we shall not cease from defending the cause and the principles we have embraced.

The day will come when we will not have to live under the shadow of fear and death, and on that historic day, the true justice of our cause will be seen.

Your Honor,

Many days and months of an unjust, cruel and horrible imprisonment have gone by!

I have sometimes wondered, what is time? And like Saint Agustin I have answered myself, "If they ask me I don't know, but if they don't ask me, I do know." Hours of solitude and hopes, of reflection about injustice and small mindedness;

eternal minutes in which memories burn bright: There are memories that burn the memory!

I take these verses by Martí for this last page that I write in the diary of my long days:

"I have lived:
It was to duty that I pledged my arms
And not once did the sun drop down behind the hills
That did not see my struggle and my victory..."
(Free verses)

And here in this courtroom I quote from the Uruguayan and world poet, Mario Benedetti:

"...victory will be there, just like me,
simply germinating"

Because, in the end, we shall rest free and victorious beneath that sun which we are denied today
Thank you

No tittle JUAN MOREIRA

Five years after our court statements

Those sentences

There I'll be, face to the Judge,
Even if in isolation I remain enclosed.

It may have been legally established, I still don't know but I believe it was; nevertheless it was a concession intended to scare us and to "torture" us some way. Suddenly, Judge Lenard allowed our presence during the sentence hearing, that is, before we had heard our own sentences. Each and every one of us expressed to our lawyers our wish to be present in the courtroom. That's how the Five could be closer than ever that Wednesday, December 12, 2001, when Gerardo was given the unjust and harsh two-life sentences plus fifteen years.

A man is gone, his freedom lost
With no sense of respect for human life…
Viciousness and deceit prevail
While truth is of no avail,
The brutal sentence a calculated act
Justice lost, no meaning in that;
My brother saw his sentence passed.

The following day it was Ramón. Gerardo was no longer with us in the courtroom, that is, physically for his soul was there. Ramón was given a life sentence plus 18 years.

Then, on Friday 14, it was René's turn; Fernando and I were there. He was given by Judge Lenard the maximum possible sentence, 15 years in prison plus that shameful ruling which clearly showed the hand of the terrorist Miami Mafia, and I quote:

"As a condition of his supervised release, the accused is prohibited from associating himself with or visiting specific places known to harbor or be the haunts of individuals or groups such as terrorists, members of organizations which advocate violence or figures of organized crime."

The lectern he held with both his hands
breathing came hard, silence the air stole;
his eyes as deep as heaven above
the challenge ahead and the truth before,
the sentence would come

indignity foretold;
his face to the right
saw the prosecutor smile,
but hate there was not
for his words came out strong
And his body was light;

The mothers were there,
Gallant, unassailable they were.
His friends like his people, the soul and the heart,
And when his saying he had he thought of his flag
And there was light.
His words like a spear

From this brother we hear;
Honor and duty, homeland and peace
My brother has served.

On Tuesday the 18th I arrived at the Court House with Fernando, but once Judge Lenard was in I was taken out, for my lawyer could not attend this hearing. How I would have liked to listen to him, too, denounce with irrefutable arguments terrorism against our country organized in South Florida, and financed and harbored by US administrations!
Fernando was sentenced to 19 years in prison.

Nine long days would pass before my sentence hearing. We were kept in isolation, each on a different floor and in different wings of the Miami Federal Detention Center. On December 27, I went to Court alone but I carried in my heart my brothers' courage and every word they had said, that's why the first words of my statement were:

"Your Honor:

"Allow me to say that I share everything that has been said here by my four brothers in this cause: Gerardo Hernández, Ramón Labañino, René González and Fernando González. They spoke with dignity and courage before this Court."

I was also accompanied by the unwavering love I feel for my people and a profound respect for truth and dignity. So, I added: "Our Court statements are based on the strict truth, on the sound principles we spouse and on the honor of the heroic people of Cuba."

Five years later I again read our Court statements only to find that every word we said is still today as strong and valid as it then was.

Of course, if we were again taken to a Court, and charged with the same immoral accusations, we would not only repeat our arguments but also add new resounding proofs to denounce that terrorism against the Cuban people is not fiction or something of the past. At this point, confessed terrorists with a long history of links with the CIA, unrepentant of their crimes and still concocting new misdeeds, walk the streets of Miami.

Some items would not be missing in a new statement:
– Everything related to the best known terrorist in the Western Hemisphere, Luis Posada Carriles, who, despite his thick record of crimes known to the US government, has only been charged of a migratory offense. Everything about this case is irrefutable proof of the Empire's double standard in its touted "war on terror."
– The notorious case of Santiago Alvarez, Posada Carriles's "right hand" and his accomplice Oswaldo Milat, for illegal possession of arms whose only destination could be terrorism against Cuba.
– And the case of Robert Ferro, an individual with a long history of terrorism, a self-proclaimed member of Alpha 66, who hid in his house a cachet of 1500 weapons, assault rifles, handguns with silencers and even grenades, among others.

Of course, they would not be able to hold a new trial against us and hide it from the world, much less from the American people, even if they used their media to silence the truth. Today, solidarity with our cause is carried forward by 286 committees in 97 countries. Those solidarity groups would be following closely anything related to us and would raise their voices and their arms in defense of righteousness as high as they already have done, where deceit and injustice cannot reach.

As comrade Ricardo Alarcón put it, it would be a Nuremberg trial for the Miami terrorist Mafia and its backers. It's for this reason that they have done and will do everything within their power to prevent this from happening.

I remember that on that December 27, while returning to the area where I was secluded, an inmate of Cuban descent came up to me; he knew the sentence already since the local television immediately released the news, so he asked me how I felt. I didn't stop to think if he was moved by good or bad intentions, I didn't care; I honestly and shortly answered him: "It's the happiest day of my life." He was puzzled; no wonder.

How could he understand that I was happy because I had denounced terrorism against my people in the den of the Miami Mafia? How could he understand that I was happy to have exposed once again the Empire's double standard in its aggression on Cuba and its so-called "war on terror?" How could he understand I was happy to have been loyal to my people and to Fidel? How could he understand it was a victory?

Those sentences were
—Sophism, infamy, rage—
Cruel sentences.

Those were cold sentences
Masking hatred.
Our solid breast of steady principles

Those bullets could not hurt.
Our axiom confirmed, their fallacies disclosed
By their actions.

We won! And those sentences we'll fight
Sparing no determination, our might.

Antonio Guerrero Rodríguez
November 4, 2006
U.S.P. Florence, Colorado

Dancing for the captives NELSON DOMÍNGUEZ

edel morales

the forest of flags

To Tony, Mirta and Maruchi

I
The voice, listening on the other end of the line,
breathes peacefully: waits, meditates, believes,
while it freely draws a mandala in its lonely cell.
The man who articulates that voice, surprised by my voice,
said: *That's what it is*, just a minute ago,
even though he doesn't know me, I don't know him,
we have never shared a beer,
a seat in the theater, a stand
in the common swarm of stadiums,
or a mere second of mutual satisfaction.

In the family house, his mother hands me a glass of fruit juice
and asks me to talk to her imprisoned son
about the life we live, this country we see, his poems
collected in a book for the first time:
his teenager's pastime made now real
in the most unpredicted and hard way.

We do not expect to hear random caustic speeches
from one or the other, because *solitude is inside oneself*
we expect nothing but gentle talk
about the strange labyrinths of the human condition

and the literary generosity of a verse:
the light shimmering in the obscure night that falls
like the century over man's world.

It is the peaceful conversation between two strangers
helping each other to remain strong,
gazing at a distant star, while they imagine
from my altitude the ups and downs of passing days,
the long battle to come, the injustices
that come along with evil and make it stronger.

II
Eight years later, on misty September evenings,
I listen to a Cesárea Evora CD and I stroll along the streets of *El Vedado*
till I reach the sea, the wall by the sea
that the city often crowds.

Life changes, the long-lasting world changes day by day,
and the people in this country that we see change too,
and there is a permanent horrifying vision on the bloody screens
of the daily TV news: once again, planes and cars explode, once again
bombs fall onto defenseless cities: In some dark corner of the world
which could be this page tomorrow or this country or this park
where young couples kiss untroubled and laugh till dawn.

It is the ascending spiral of fear and outrage that burns it all
and ignites hatred and grows with the century,
in a violent clash of fundamentalisms that darkens it all
and shows its claws and contradicts and denies and censures
and forgets and kills all signs of breathing and life
under the hermetic shadow of the condemned towers.
It is fear, the kingdom of fear that crushes any possible choice,
before and after death and light.

I walk along the seashore humming a love song
on these misty September evenings:
I am trying to find a device to save my soul.
With their naked voice, their voice of Africa, grateful gift from their sister,
Cesárea Evora and Antonio Guerrero lead me toward the forest of black flags

(a long line of severed lives) fluttering firmly against evil,
spelling out in their waving a state of necessity.

III

I never thought it would happen, but I have seen the greatest words
crawling meekly at the tyrant's feet, bound to the neck
until they could hardly breathe: peace, freedom, democracy…
declares categorically the mediocre barbarian while he types the code
or pushes the button to open the floodgates to death;
I have seen the smart bombs explode in a crowd
and clotted blood stuck to the walls of an ice-cream parlor.
I have seen the arrogant troops of power parade before my eyes
and justice hijacked and inverted in the courts.
I have seen the battlements of an empire cracked by the flapping of a butterfly's wings.
And I have seen the waves produced with the definitive changing of an age.

I am again listening to Cesárea Evora's songs
(an unforgettable present from Maruchi in Mirta's house)
and I remember Tony's deliberate voice on the other end of the line;
I go back to the sea, by myself, to the seawall, where crowds
become faces quite often and become shouts and music and presence
in this city targeted by the enemy.
I am again walking immersed in thought next to the forest of flags,
to feel the pain and the strength that lie in my memory,
to find the cause, to dream of the return, to beg in silence
for my motherland and *humanity's full dignity*.

No tittle — ALICIA LEAL

francisco lópez sacha

On a foothill, under the Boston sky, Benjamin Franklin is flying a kite.
It's one of his common scientific experiments.
A man who watches him pulling and letting out the reel of thread,
and taking time in that sort of game, asks him,
"And what's that good for?"
and Franklin replies with a smile:
"What's a child good for? Well, he'll grow to be a man."

ANONYMOUS SOUND

Last night, writer Osmani Oduardo told me a story from his trip to Honduras and I want to relate it as a witness, even if it's not a personal experience. A Cuban doctor, his leg swollen from a snake bite, lies in pain on a stretcher in a medical field post, waiting for the antidote that will safe his life. The place, an outpost of Cuba's medical mission in the jungle, is located half an hour from the nearest hospital, in a rough mountainous region. The doctor moans in pain. He is pale and sweat is running cold down his spine. His ankle is bloody. There is only one vial in the reserve and he's about to be given the shot when a boy is rushed in by his father. The boy is dirty; he's crying in pain from a similar bite and the nurse accommodates him on the other stretcher. The doctor still in pain watches the child and with an authoritative gesture indicates that the only antidote be given to the boy. A heavy silence reigns under the concrete roof, in the rarefied atmosphere of the medical outpost. The assistant looks at him hesitatingly. The doctor bites his lips and insists pounding on the stretcher with clenched fists. Half an hour later, just as expected, when the doctor is already gasping for air and about to die, they come in with another vial from the hospital. I cannot imagine that half hour in the harsh silence of the mountain; a man is adrift leaning on a rough stretcher knowing death is certain if the antidote doesn't come in on time; this man has decided to die, to give up his life to save that of a child, a perfect unknown. I cannot imagine that excruciating pain, the ankle swelling, the foot growing rigid, the small marks where the snakes' teeth sank now covered with bloody foam, and a cold air flowing up his blood stream. That long wait can be as exhausting as death itself; the doctor, who knows the symptoms, is starting to feel cold all over, the numbness crawling up his leg and the stabbing pain, while he looks out of the corner of his eye to see his foot strangely livid. It can take the poison twenty to thirty minutes to make the journey through the blood flow and reach the chest, the central nervous system and the heart. How long can he really wait? How much time if there is really something like time? If he died, the child would go back to the mountain, the jungle, taking perhaps as a memory –a child's vague feeling— the doctor's death rattle, even if one day he'd know the truth. Will that memory matter later, and that conscience, that courage, the fulfillment of the professional and human duty transcending even oneself? The doctor has perhaps decided it should matter, or perhaps he hasn't even thought of it and it's a dark, basic force that drives him to give that order, to defend the boy's life rather than his own. But a child, what's a child good for?

The foot has now a grayish blue color. From the depth of the jungle come strange, distant noises. Somebody covers the light coming through the window panel to the improvised space in the field post. Somebody is walking impatiently. How can you measure, how, the courage of that man who is lying on a stretcher, soaking in sweat, waiting in the anonymous sound of a humid and near and shimmering jungle, alone with a life that is leaving him? Where is our limit? Is it in the risk? Is it in our conscience? Is it in the margin for error? Or, is it in time? Is it in time precisely, the same that is sometimes elusive and that hurts us, sometimes? Is it in ethics? Is it in politics? Is it in the future recognition of this action by his comrades? Is it in the agony of death, almost 1250 miles away from Cuba, his eyes glassy from the pain but still in silence, with that swelling which is already numbing his thigh, while his tongue is dry, and he keeps staring at the nurse who had provisionally made a tourniquet with gauze to prevent the poison from circulating slowly up his crotch and to his chest preventing his breathing?

I don't really know how to measure this action. Here I lose track of words and my dark inkwell cannot get there, nothing gets there. It's just an image that we can hardly think of or describe but which comes from deep inside, from the glassy staring eyes, from the certainty of this grown man who no longer fits anywhere, that he has made a final choice because he cannot betray his mission.

It's this and something else that I can't define, even if I try.

It would be too little to say that this man is a hero. Perhaps we lack a word that can describe his gesture and the word hero might also dissolve in the pen just as when we write on a tarred paper with a thick ink and the ink gets stuck and doesn't flow. Perhaps there is a new word, a still unimagined and unspent substantive, one that can express this strange sliding to the red, when the limits to courage expand and all of man's qualities converge for a second in one decision.

Yet, for that man to last after he's given the shot of antidote, and for him to breathe, and again to stand up, with his head still hanging and a nauseating feeling twisting his stomach, to feel this rejoicing which I can't express either, for I haven't experienced it; and for this man to clean his sweat and to stand up, I mean, for this man to exist and to be there tomorrow or the day after, and for him to be able to walk again under the deadly sound of the jungle, carrying his backpack through the ages-old harshness of the stones and the mountains of Honduras so that the humble people who live in adobe houses and painted wagons may live; and for the children to be good for growing into men, not far from death which is inevitable but far from the danger of a useless life; for other men like him to continue to be born everywhere, even for me to be able to write this pages in peace, in Cuba —because after all I feel as innocent as that child and I only chose what I think is fair, among other things my right to preserve my conscience— that is, for other men of his same lineage who have felt the need to defend my life and that of millions of other human beings like myself, men whose faces would hardly be recognized in a crowd or in a mass rally, for example, beyond the reiteration of their names which are by now in everybody's mouth, and for them to be known in the collective imagery as the Five Heroes, while they really are human beings distinguishable from others only by their faces, their gestures, their manners and something that makes them single and unique persons, men that cannot be repeated and that we shall never be able to define, such men, I say, warned us timely of a greater danger involving the security and the destiny of an entire people, and they did it, naturally, for me, for you, for that doctor, and even for that child whom he saved.

If they are now unjustly kept in various prisons in the United States, if they cannot see each other and suffer from solitude and from the ominous silence of confinement; if for eight years they have been serving an unjust and illegal sentence, which even the judges rejected when they learned of a rigged trial, and which is also rejected by millions and millions of honest people in the world, a brutal sentence that hardly allows them to meet their children or to fully communicate with their families because the US administration refuses to issue them visas to enter that country; and if they are still in prison due to our enemy's cruelty and its illegal and arbitrary actions, and if they are, after all, innocents of all the charges falsely brought against them, albeit they're not innocent of loving, and of acting accordingly, even at the risk of their lives, then they are heroes, even though the word cannot offer a better description of their actions, and there is no other word to define them, as I cannot describe the doctor's action or the suffering of a child.

April 11, 2007

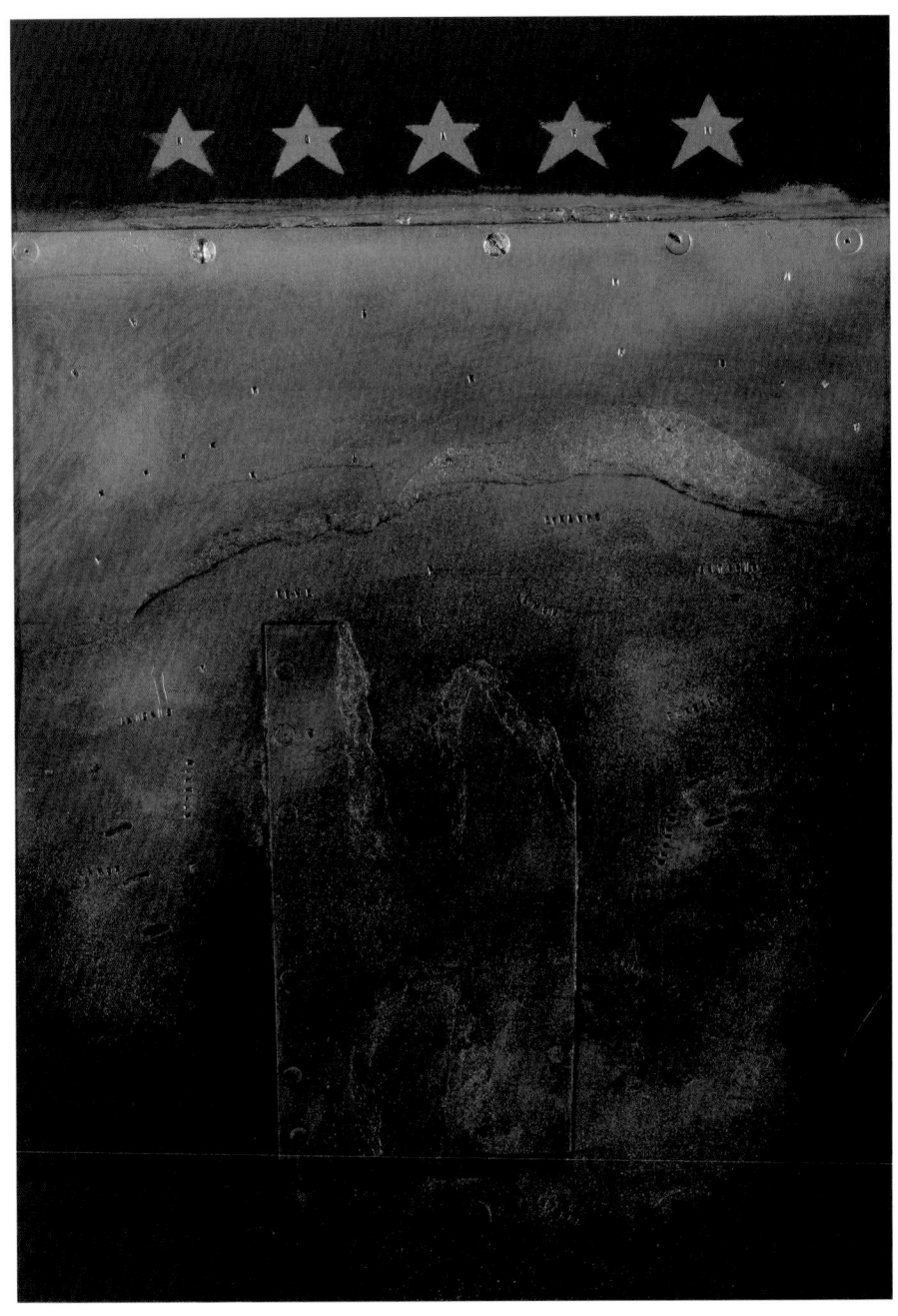

No tittle Manuel Comas

cintio vitier

antonio

And the poem for you, poet. Injustice
Could not omit you in its revenge:
she knows, like lucid indecency
what love amounts for beauty.

But she does not care. The mission commences
believing hope is being chained,
believing greed is prostituting the words,
and tilting the balance in favor of merchants.

In turn, you have your son's laughter,
Your mother's strength, and the word
of the one whom forever told Cubans:

Only the impossible will be possible.
Cheers, Antonio. Your speech is forging
the already invincible stanza of the five.

No tittle					Juan Moreira

CUBA NEEDS EYES AND EARS IN FLORIDA

Edward Atkeson, Division General in the US Army, former chief of the Intelligence Planning Office.

Regarding the evidence, the General's response to the defense attorneys was:

—As you examined the evidence, did you find any instructions to these people for getting classified material?
—No.
—Did you ever find any instructions to the agents to obtain material harmful to the United States?
—No.

THE WITNESS RODOLFO FROMETA DECIDES NOT TO TAKE THE FIFTH AMMENDMENT AND TESTIFY ON HIS ACTIVITIES WITH THE TERRORIST GROUPS ALPHA 66 AND COMMANDOS F-4. IN HIS TESTIMONY HE ADMITS, AMONG OTHER THINGS:

- The paramilitary training of both groups in South Florida;
- The armed raids against Cuba from South Florida;
- That he was arrested on June 1994 as he tried to purchase C-4 explosive, antitank rifles and Stinger antiaircraft rockets from an FBI undercover agent. After his arrest he cut a deal with the South Florida Federal Prosecution office to admit being guilty in exchange for only one year of house arrest, and was released on parole to await the trial.

He would soon continue with his terrorist activities.

The witness for the defense Debbie McMullen, an investigator with the Public Defense office, introduces in Court the evidence obtained from the communications taken from the five defendants that show the true reason for their presence in Miami:

TO MONITOR AND FOLLOW THE TERRORIST ACTIVITIES AGAINST CUBA ORIGINATED IN THAT CITY

Testimony by Debbie McMullen, April 12, 2001

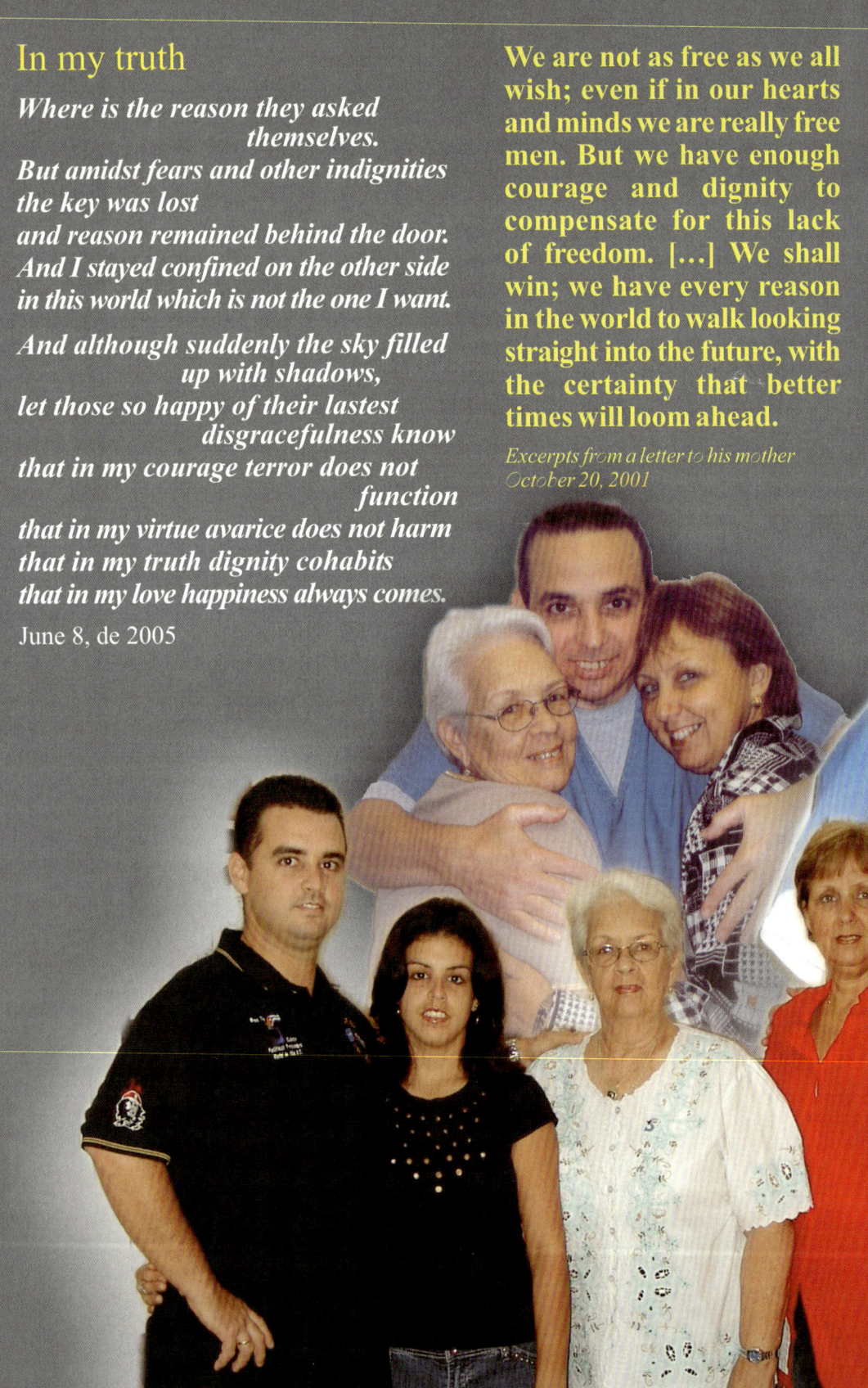

In my truth

*Where is the reason they asked
         themselves.
But amidst fears and other indignities
the key was lost
and reason remained behind the door.
And I stayed confined on the other side
in this world which is not the one I want.*

*And although suddenly the sky filled
         up with shadows,
let those so happy of their lastest
         disgracefulness know
that in my courage terror does not
                    function
that in my virtue avarice does not harm
that in my truth dignity cohabits
that in my love happiness always comes.*

June 8, de 2005

We are not as free as we all wish; even if in our hearts and minds we are really free men. But we have enough courage and dignity to compensate for this lack of freedom. [...] We shall win; we have every reason in the world to walk looking straight into the future, with the certainty that better times will loom ahead.

*Excerpts from a letter to his mother
October 20, 2001*

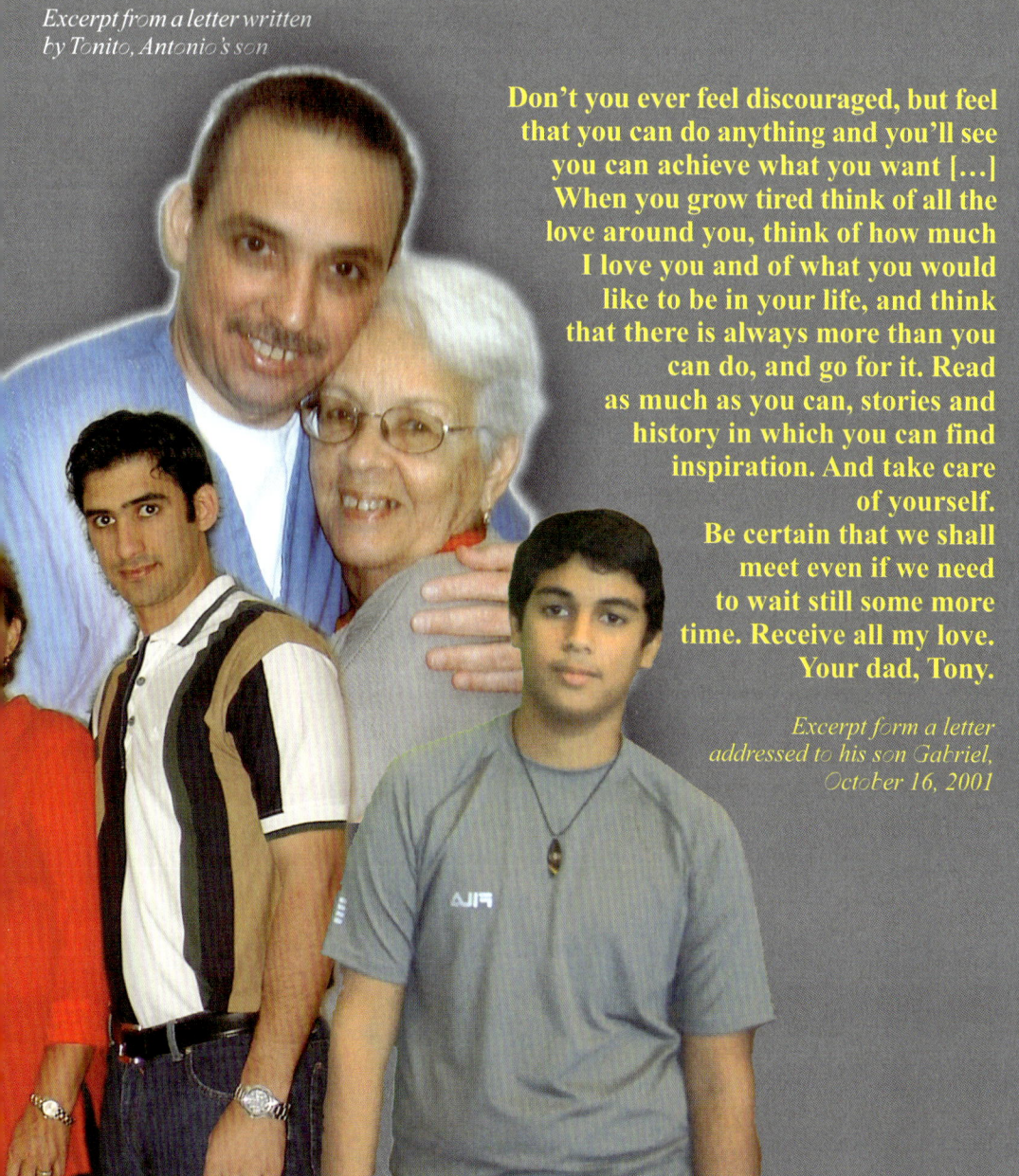

Daddy will be back.

He's always interested about my health and school. There is this great love and affection between us. I feel pride, admiration and respect for him. I know he will be back because he's innocent; he is a man of honor and a patriot [...] he is a cultivated man, well trained, intelligent, playful, a man who likes to tell stories and to laugh. When he is upset he speaks in short and cutting phrases, but he's always honest [...] he doesn't know hate and he never forgets those who help him.

Excerpt from a letter written by Tonito, Antonio's son

Don't you ever feel discouraged, but feel that you can do anything and you'll see you can achieve what you want [...] When you grow tired think of all the love around you, think of how much I love you and of what you would like to be in your life, and think that there is always more than you can do, and go for it. Read as much as you can, stories and history in which you can find inspiration. And take care of yourself.
Be certain that we shall meet even if we need to wait still some more time. Receive all my love.
Your dad, Tony.

Excerpt form a letter addressed to his son Gabriel, October 16, 2001

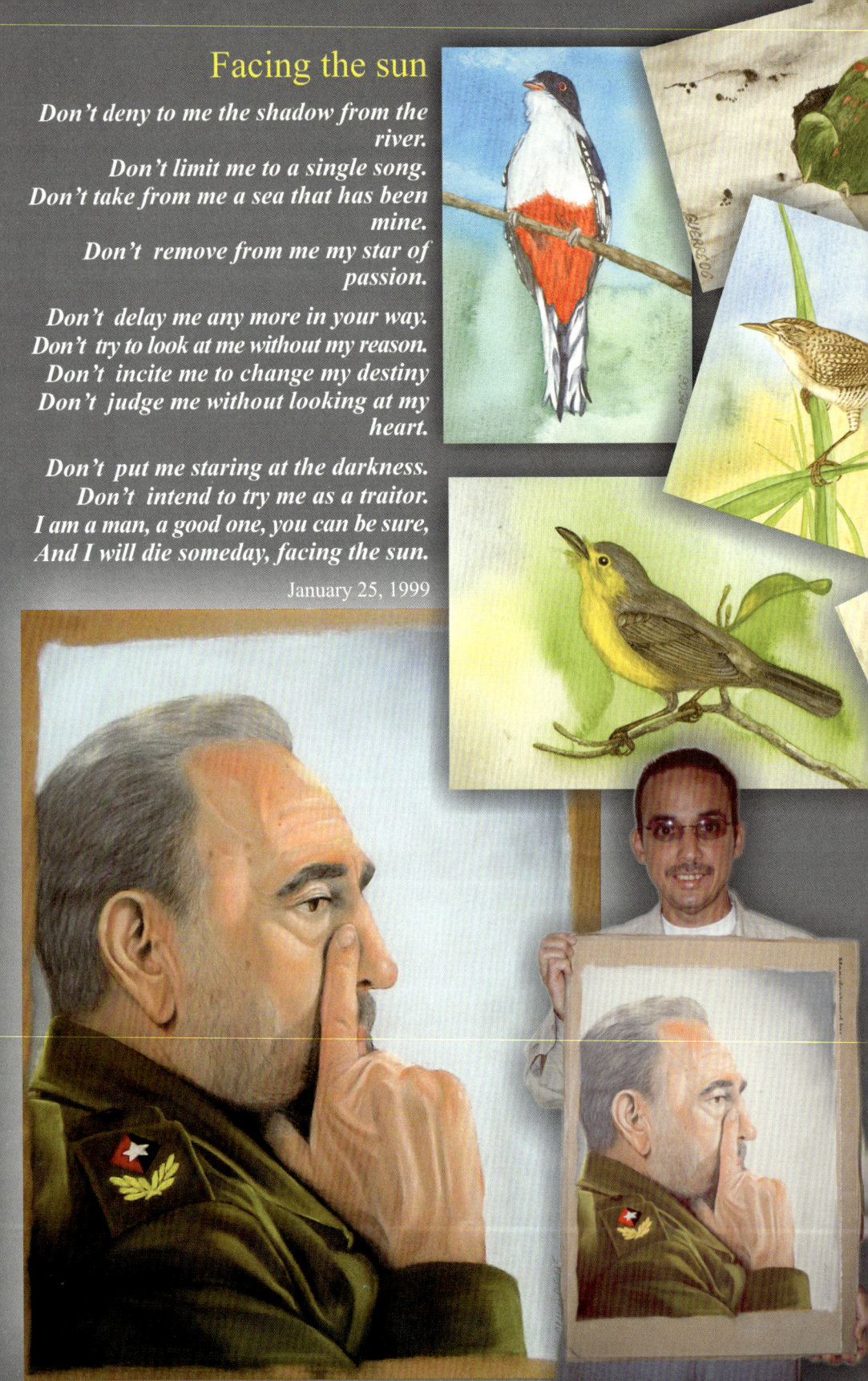

Facing the sun

Don't deny to me the shadow from the river.
Don't limit me to a single song.
Don't take from me a sea that has been mine.
Don't remove from me my star of passion.

Don't delay me any more in your way.
Don't try to look at me without my reason.
Don't incite me to change my destiny
Don't judge me without looking at my heart.

Don't put me staring at the darkness.
Don't intend to try me as a traitor.
I am a man, a good one, you can be sure,
And I will die someday, facing the sun.

January 25, 1999

The fourth pass

*Prison guard who guards these four walls,
four times per day, sounding your keys
you pass in a big hurry, by my door
with the weight of the tedium in your grim face.
Three are obligated:
breakfast time, lunch time and dinner time,
and the fourth is when yon want to,
or you decide
to give me my weekly telephone call,
or to offer me a razor to shave my beard,
or to change the dirty sheets,
or that you pass with you little flashlight at
midnight and waking me
stuns my dream with your ambiguous glance.*

*Prison guard who guards these four walls,
four dates are marked in the book of life:
our birth, marriage,
the date of our death and the fourth is
the day that we mark a point of departure,
an important guideline.
I am conserving this one
for the day when you come to my door
in an unusual fourth pass
and say to me: PACK!*

Every painting made me feel like walking on our free soil, on our beautiful countryside.

For a just cause

*Suppose that you have not had the way
to confess to people who you are,
to people whom you miss and love more,
to those who dignify your flag.*

*Suppose that you have no attempt at least,
dedicate yourself to something more than
your debts,
deprived your life of pleasures,
that to be useful is your only chimera.*

*From that place and with that assumption
imagine yourself walking on the earth
given to peace and justice.*

*You will see there is no greater satisfaction
than to try to shun some war,
although always you have need of a caress.*

I will not defraud you

To my father

I attend on this day to your name
on this singular day of summer
austere, resolved, clear, faraway.
If I am so firm, father, do not be
surprised.

I am not that one, but today I am
the man
that your dreams lead by the hand.
I am not a child, but clean and sane,
to my firmness I put your renown.

I will return

I will return and say to life
I have come back to be your confidant.
From north to south I will deliver to the people
the part of my love hidden within me.

I will sprinkle the immeasurable happiness
of one who knows to laugh unpretentiously.

From east to west I will raise my countenance
with goodness forever promised.
For where the wind has whipped, harsh and strong,
I will go looking for the leaves on the path.

I will unite their dreams of such fortune
they cannot fly away in a whirlwind.
I will sing my songs to destiny
and with my voice, make death tremble.

June 24, 1999

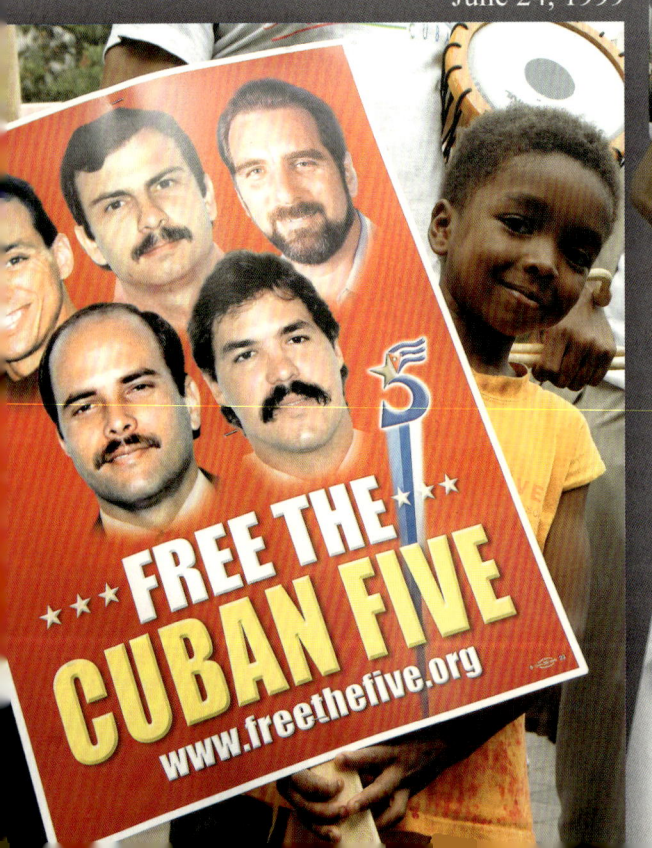

The fight against terrorism is the defendants' motivation and motivations are not to be discussed in front of the Jury.

Official documents of the trial. Prosecution's motion, 2000

The first duty of any self-respecting person is to his or her country. Throughout the years of my imprisonment, I will always carry with me the dignity I have learned from my people and their history.

Fernando

marta rojas

MY TEACHER, MY LOVE

It was a journey to nothing. The prison is in the middle of nowhere, in a flat area with a blanket of snow in winter; only once in so many years I have seen it green with a corn plantation. At intervals I can see from the car the towering pine trees, upright just like Fernando. The houses, though isolated, bring to mind the warmth of a home that he filled, in a different landscape, when we were together and he said, "You look pretty in your uniform," a working uniform with a simple blue and white polka-dot blouse, and a blue skirt. A few more miles in this car that I took in the Ridge Motor Inn and I'll be there. But before, I'll see the isolated houses of farmers, and later some monotonous buildings, probably the housing for the workers of the prison where he is confined, serving an undeserved sentence. He is innocent of the charges brought against him. Who is condemned for preventing crime and destruction? Well, he is, and his four comrades, and nine years have passed. Three of them, —according to the culprits of the true crime— will have to serve two full lives and more.

Ultimately, a building shows in front of my eyes, an old building compared to the new American constructions. It's the Oxford prison, a place so far to the north of the United States that it is close to Canada. Oxford sounds like a university but it's a brutal center, just like all prisons are.

I know by now what lies behind this first bloc of buildings: the compartmentalized living quarters or *dorms* where the inmates live; it's an euphemism to call them *dorms* for in my revolutionary culture we speak of dorms in the students' boarding schools, while these are the opposite of that culture, except for Fernando's limited space, very tightly closed with iron bars, where he constantly reads and writes about the literary, political, philosophical and anthropological books he now prefers, especially the latter. In a letter of more than ten pages that I received in Cuba, he offered his comments on the book *Armas, gérmenes y acero*, saying many good things about it but also waging some very strong criticisms. Of course, he suggested or rather challenged me to find the book, read it and share my views with him. I read to someone his comments on that book and the person suggested that I make a copy of his comments and his criticisms on the works that he's interested in and reads in prison to have them published. Such a book could be a compilation of his comments on other books. Perhaps that person is right.

I'm almost at the end of my journey. Here is the wire fence and the smoke, probably from a fireplace since it is winter. I'll walk in: just a hug and a kiss at the beginning and the end of the visit, once a year; on a Saturday, Sunday and Monday of one month in a year. Then, it's back to the beginning; to start all over again with the paper work, always uncertain if there will be a next time.

First I'm searched under surveillance from a TV camera. My hands almost put under the X rays to detect any chemical substance…finally we hug and kiss. We are face to face and we start talking, our words initially overlapping for we want to speak at the same time as our hearts beat at the same pace. Fernando, sitting in front of me, understands what happens. He has always been more rational; I'm more emotional. To cap it all I can't help a tear running down my face. He says, "Try not to think of the time we won't be seeing each other; think of this moment and try to remember it." He's right, why waste this moment on tears.

I would want to tell him that he's always been my teacher, but we have so much to say and so little time. However, silence is another way to communicate; gazing into each other's eyes, looking intently. He can no longer call me "skinny" because I quit smoking and I've put on weight. Then, he advises me to exercise more, like he does in winter when the snow would not allow him to jog outdoors, in the time allotted for that, and he goes up and down the stairs of the gym many times to keep in good shape.

The day I told him I had moved he asked me a thousand questions. He wanted to know everything there was to know about the apartment, every inch of it. When I told him, he wanted to know about the walls, what I'd be hanging on the walls, because we both like the framed prints of famous Cuban paintings, and some wood carvings, like those made by a craftswoman whose work I'm familiar with. We used to live with his mother, Magaly Llort, my mother-in-law, but now she lives with a grand-daughter and I'm preparing our love nest because I'm sure we'll be together again, and I want that every corner of our apartment is arranged according to our taste; I know his taste. We know our tastes.

I cannot help these reflections, even in this short time. I see him in front of me – a table between us two and a row of similar tables and chairs in a rectangular room— and I wonder how a government that approved a law authorizing torture of an alleged culprit, without evidence, a government that orders torturing in any jail, even in the Naval Base located in the usurped territory of Guantanamo, as well as in Iraq and many other places in the world; how can such a government that protects a terrorist, actually many terrorists, condemn somebody who was fighting terrorism practiced by that same government —as part of its established policy— against my homeland, Cuba, and there are many examples of this. There is no answer to my question; I can't find one.

I don't speak about this with Fernando, my teacher. But, as always, he seems to guess my deepest feelings and then he writes things like this: "After all, I should thank Karl Marx for his writings on political economics that allowed me to get close to you to explain it; it might not have had the revolutionary impact he expected from his theory buy it unquestionably revolutionized my life, even if I did not court you reading *The Capital*."

That's how we met. We were neighbors but we hardly crossed paths. His sister was a friend of mine but I hardly knew him before I needed somebody to help me with my economic class and his sister Martha volunteered to talk with Fernando whom she said knew a lot about it. And so, the student fell in love with the teacher and the teacher feel in love with the student, and step by step we grew close; as I read somewhere about love and sacrifice, love grows stronger when it is anointed with sacrifice. But this sacrifice need not be so unfair and extensive, because he and I, we are suffering for five people, or rather six, because Magaly Llort is important, very important, for she is already 68 years old, although she is strong in body and soul.

The most recent interview was the worst, second only to the first. I had entertained the illusion that the Atlanta Court of Appeals had already solved part of the problem, that in a week he would be home and see what I had done in the apartment, although I had not hung yet the framed prints of the paintings on the wall, or found a place for the wood carving. But, he would do it himself, I thought; he would open the holes on the wall and meticulously insert the pieces of wood to hammer the nail into, perhaps he would get some steel nails which are better and prevent oxidation; he would take measures and hang them at the exact place, which I can't do. Then, the unexpected happened! I was depressed during the visit. However, even in such a hostile environment, a man who is only 43 years old —who as he humorously said already carries a tonsure on the back of his head and some gray hair in his beard which he grew in winter and showed to me in a letter with a drawing of himself that he sent me— this man tells me, "Don't you think about what's happening to us, think of this moment," and he teaches me a lesson in *social communication* as he analyzes our case succinctly in the short time of a prison visit. Of course, he's right, our battle should not cease but I should bear in mind that people in this country are mostly inclined to follow events on television and a case "like our case" has no place in television, at least not yet. He cheers me up to continue working for an understanding of the case and to build solidarity everywhere because that can help.

Then I thought of an American, Bill, and I was grateful; and I thought of Gloria and other friends over there, and I ended up looking for a picture that Bill took of me.

When Fernando was transferred from prison, a few years ago, he took it off the cell wall but in the new place he couldn't hang it in front of him, nor did it fit in his album, so he sent it back. To me it's just a picture, a symbol of solidarity. Perhaps I could have it reproduced in a smaller format because he has told me it was his best company. Bill made a photo in which my eyes seemed to be looking at him wherever he hung the picture, and so it kept him company. Then he says, and I know, I too can guess it, "There is no force strong enough to abate our love."

Beloved — ROBERTO FABELO

Defense statement presented by Fernando González Llort at the sentencing hearing held tuesday, december 18, 2001

Your Honor:

I share with my comrades who have preceded me here in their recognition and gratitude for the professional behavior of Richard, the translators who have worked so efficiently, and the U.S. Marshals.

I also share in what has been expressed here by every one of my brothers at their sentencing hearings. I feel honored by the friendship of these comrades and brothers, who received their unjust sentences with such courage and dignity.

I also want to express my gratitude for the professional work of the attorneys representing the five of us, particularly Joaquín Méndez and the south Florida district public defenders office.

If it were not very clear to me that the fanaticism, hatred and irrationality felt towards Cuba are generated and stimulated by only a minority segment of the Cuban-American community living here, I would not have agreed to be represented by a member of that community. His professional approach to this case shows that, contrary to what those who control the Hispanic media would like to make everyone believe, with their stridently anti-Cuban stance, the majority of the Cuban-American community in Florida has a rational attitude towards their country of origin, even when they hold opinions that differ with the government of Cuba.

This is also showed by the fact that hundreds of thousands of Cuban-Americans travel to Cuba every year, and send money to their relatives there.

Those who believe that Cuban radio stations in Miami and the extremist Cuban organizations based here represent the point of view of the majority of Cuban-Americans living in this city have fallen into the trap set by this extremist and minority-based yet economically powerful sector. They try to sell an image of unity and pretend they represent the sentiments of hundreds of thousands of Cubans who live here, when this is not the case.

Your Honor:

I initially thought the prosecution would come to this courtroom today to request that I be sentenced to one year of probation. After all, that was what this same District Attorney's Office offered Mr. Frómeta when he bought a Stinger missile, C-4 explosive, grenades and other weapons from an undercover government agent. It did not even matter that Mr. Frómeta confessed to the undercover agent himself his terrorist intentions and the murderous, unscrupulous use that would be made of these materials.

But then I thought it over again, and I realized that I would have to be dreaming to expect the same kind of treatment from the District Attorney's Office. After all, I am a Cuban from over there, from the island, and so when it comes to sentencing me, all kinds of considerations come into play. These include the total ignorance as to what Cuba really is, and the hatred and irrationality towards my country stimulated by an extremist sector that controls what is said here about Cuba while silencing any other, more rational opinions expressed.

While our trial was underway in this courtroom, Esteban Ventura Novo passed away in Miami, and I am bringing this up because I believe it is symbolic of something.

Esteban Ventura Novo was one of the chiefs of police under the Fulgencio Batista dictatorship in Cuba, before the triumph of the Revolution. He was responsible for the torture, murder and vanishing of dozens of young people in the Cuban capital. And all of this happened with the consent and support of the U.S. government, led at the time by Eisenhower.

When the revolutionary government took power in Cuba, Ventura Novo and others like him, perpetrators of crimes against the Cuban people, were received and sheltered by this country's government. Many of them were advised, directed and financed by U.S. intelligence agencies, in their dirty war against a government that obviously enjoyed and continues to enjoy the support of its people.

This marked the beginning of a long history of aggression against Cuba in every field of the country's economic and social life. A history in which economic warfare, biological warfare, and psychological warfare through propaganda and the threat of military attack, have combined with terrorism, sabotage, paramilitary actions and attempts on the lives of the political leaders of the Revolution, almost all of them originating in south Florida.

The prosecution will say that this is just Cuba's propaganda and paranoia. I wonder if they would have the nerve to go to Cuba and say that to the mothers, spouses and children of those who have lost their lives as victims of these acts of aggression. Such statements on the part of the prosecution demonstrate their lack of human sensitivity and their inability to put themselves in someone else's shoes.

The activities of the Cuban-American terrorist and paramilitary groups based in South Florida have been used as instruments of this country's foreign policy towards Cuba through their direct organization by U.S. government agencies, the support given by these agencies to the extremist groups that perpetrate the acts, or by simply allowing them to operate without real persecution or with benevolent treatment when someone has actually been arrested.

The terrorist groups of the Miami Cuban ultra-right wing were created, trained and financed by the CIA. This has always been abundantly clear to the Cuban people. If there are still any doubts among those present in this courtroom, they need merely take a look at the documents declassified by the United States government itself in 1997 and 1998, which clearly expose the decisions adopted by this country's top leaders.

One of these documents refers to a meeting attended by high-level officials, headed up by the vice president at the time, Richard Nixon. This was the meeting at which the so-called "Program of Covert Action Against the Castro Regime" was approved. In a memorandum on the meeting, one of the participants, General Goodpaster, noted, "The President said that he knows of no better plan for dealing with this situation. The great problem is leakage and breach of security. Everyone must be prepared to swear that he (Eisenhower) has not heard of it. (...) He said our hand should not show in anything that is done."

I ask myself: what can we expect 30 or 40 years from now, when they decide to declassify documents on what is happening today?

The majority of Cuban-Americans who remain active in terrorist actions against Cuba today, 40 years later, are well known to the United States security agencies, because they belong to those agencies, and have learned everything they know about technical means and working methods from them.

Their ties with the far right fundamentalists of U.S. politics have led to their apparent involvement in the darkest episodes of this country's recent history: the assassination of President Kennedy, the Watergate scandal, the murders of Orlando Letelier and Ronnie Moffit, and the clandestine supply of arms to the Nicaraguan Contras, in violation of the laws passed by Congress. Their activities have always run counter to the interests of the American people.

Perhaps it is their complicity with and loyalty to that political sector of this society that guarantees them impunity for their actions against Cuba, and provides them with the certitude that their activities will be overlooked by the authorities, and that political pressure will exerted in their favor in the event that they are caught. The facts prove this to be so.

Such is the case of Luis Posada Carriles and Orlando Bosh, both with long histories of ties with the CIA. Together, they were the masterminds behind the blowing up in mid-flight of a Cuban commercial airplane on October 6, 1976, an act that caused the deaths of 73 innocent people.

Orlando Bosh lives as a free man in this community thanks to the parole granted by former president George Herbert Bush, despite the fact that officials from this country's own Department of Justice consider him a dangerous and notorious terrorist.

The recommendations and pressures of Florida Republican representative Ileana Ros-Lehtinen played a major role in the granting of this presidential parole to Orlando Bosh. She is, therefore, a defender and protector of terrorists.

The evidence submitted here by the defense —documents known to the FBI and introduced during the trial— prove that Orlando Bosh has not ceased to conspire to commit terrorist acts against Cuba from Miami. But, he has not been arrested.

This past August 22, a full-page ad was published in *The Miami Herald*, in which a so-called "Cuban Patriotic Forum" established among its principles that it recognizes and supports the use of any methods in the struggle against Cuba. One of the signatories of this declaration was Orlando Bosh. Such is the impunity of his acts.

The case of Posada Carriles is even more shameful. Having escaped from a Venezuelan jail, where he was being held for his participation in the blowing up of a Cuban commercial plane that killed 73 innocent civilians, he surfaced in Central America with a new false name, working under the orders of none other than Lieutenant Colonel Oliver North. North, of course, was the official from the Reagan administration's Security Council involved in the so-called Iran-Contra scandal, subsequently investigated by a special prosecutor.

All of this is documented and known to the U.S. security services. They also know that it was the Cuban-American National Foundation that financed and organized Posada Carriles' escape from a Venezuelan jail.

Today, Luis Posada Carriles and three other Cuban-Americans resident in Miami, all with long histories of involvement in terrorist acts against Cuba and also in the U.S. territory, are currently held in detention in Panama. They were arrested for their participation in a plot to blow up the university auditorium in Panamá City with C-4 explosive while President Fidel Castro was meeting there with thousands of Panamanian students.

These terrorists imprisoned in Panama are receiving support from Miami. Money is being collected through public fundraising campaigns for their defense, with the use of Cuban-American radio stations. Pressure is being exerted on the Panamanian authorities and the legal defense of these terrorists is being arranged, while conditions are created for an eventual escape. There is no need to add that here, on the radio and in the press controlled by the Cubans of the far right, they are considered patriots, and not lowly terrorists, which is what they really are.

All of this is taking place in full view of this country's authorities.

A lengthy account could be given of the entire terrorist and paramilitary activities and the attempts on the lives of Cuba's political leaders organized from south Florida. With regard to the latter, in 1975 the Church Commission of the U.S. Senate compiled a partial list of those in which the CIA was directly involved, and for which it even resorted to members of organized crime. Such is their lack of ethics.

What choice do the Cuban people have for defending their sovereignty and their security?

All of us here in this courtroom are familiar with the concept of "probable cause", used, among other things, for authorizing the use of certain means and methods in criminal investigations, for carrying out searches, making arrests, and so on. Who in the U.S. government can state here in this courtroom that over these last 42 years, there has not been "probable cause" to justify and legally support the investigation of actions initiated or financed from south Florida against Cuba?

In the course of our trial, the prosecution, in a blatant show of hypocrisy, threatened to use the R.I.C.O. Act against witnesses for the defense if they testified in this courtroom. Their goal was to keep the terrorist activities in which these gentlemen had participated from coming to light.

The R.I.C.O. Act, passed by Congress fundamentally to fight organized crime, has been in force for over 20 years. However, it has never been applied to a single one of the terrorist groups based here in Miami, although the government has all the information required to do so.

Here you have an example that there are in fact laws that would allow for these individuals and groups to be criminally prosecuted.

The problem is that, at the very least, there has been no political will to do so. If that political will did exist, many of the terrorist organizations that publicly operate offices in Miami would have been forced to shut down and their members sent to prison.

This is just a brief summary of the reality that the Cuban people have had to face and with which they have had to live throughout more than 40 years. The Cuban people have the right to defend themselves, because up until now the U.S. government, which is responsible for enforcing the laws of this country and passing new laws if they are needed to combat criminal acts, has done very little or nothing to stop these activities against Cuba.

It was within this context that we reached the decade of the 90s. Cuba was facing the most critical economic situation in the last 40 years, fundamentally as a result of external factors.

The terrorist groups based in Miami and allied with the far right of U.S. politics believed that the time had come to deal the definitive coup de grâce to Cuba's revolutionary government. Thus, political actions and terrorist acts were simultaneously stepped up.

The Cuban-American National Foundation (CANF) became the Cuban community's most influential organization, due to its economic resources and the influence it exerted over key politicians in the United States' government structure.

Its strategy was to work towards the adoption in Congress of measures aimed at economically strangling the Cuban people, with the false hope that this would lead them to rise up against the revolutionary government, while at the same time, a wave of terrorist attacks against Cuba would be organized and financed from Miami, with the goal of damaging the already recovering economy.

This wave of terrorist acts against tourism facilities in Cuba was financed and organized by the CANF. The head terrorist, Luis Posada Carriles, acknowledged to *The New York Times* his responsibility for the planning of these attacks and the financing of them with money from that organization. In articles published by the newspaper on July 12 and 13, 1998, Posada Carriles tacitly admitted that he functioned as the armed wing of the CANF.

In that same interview, he explained that the U.S. authorities had made no effort to question him about the terrorist attacks on hotels in Cuba, and that he attributed this lack of action to his longstanding relationship with them. He literally said:

"As you can see (...) the FBI and the CIA don't bother me, and I'm neutral with them. Whenever I can help them, I do."

During the following days, the eminently anti-Cuban press in Miami would work to erase from the minds of the Cuban community the statements and serious claims published by *The New York Times*, pushing them out of the local media with something that constitutes an obsession within this community: a purported illness afflicting President Fidel Castro. It did not matter that the story was a hoax, and was dispelled within a matter of days. It had accomplished its objective of making the general public forget what had been published in *The New York Times* and the potential repercussions of the statements made to that paper by Posada Carriles.

But the FBI and other U.S. authorities should not have forgotten since the above-mentioned articles were published on July 12 and 13 and exactly 26 days before the publication of those articles an official U.S. delegation, which included FBI officers, visited Havana where it was provided with extensive information, filmed footage and tape recordings containing evidence of the participation of the CANF and its top leaders in the organization and financing of terrorist acts against Cuba. Many of these materials were introduced by the defense as evidence in this case.

More than three years later, Cuba is still waiting for any FBI action to arrest any of the individuals involved.

On October 26, 1990, Mr. Angel Berlingueri, a FBI special agent from the Miami office at the time, was a guest on the "Round Table" radio show broadcast by WAQI, or "Radio Mambí". Coincidentally, this same agent participated in my arrest eight years later, and would subsequently testify in this courtroom.

He was a guest on the same radio station, with the same host and on the same show normally used to raise funds for actions against Cuba, for the defense of terrorists, and as a forum for anti-Cuban propaganda and political activity characterized by fanaticism.

That is where this FBI special agent appeared.

It is striking that in his comments and explanations to the public about the supposed activities of agents working for the Cuban government in south Florida, there is no mention of anything related to the national security of the United States. There is, however, acknowledgement of the fact that there are groups here in Miami plotting to overthrow the Cuban government. This violates the Neutrality Act, although it is clear that this issue was not brought up during the show.

On that very same radio show, this FBI agent acknowledged that actions and attacks against the Cuban government are perpetrated from Miami, and that the goal of the Cuban government is to remain informed of these plans. To top it all, the FBI agent bid farewell to his listeners by informing them that "we are fighting and we have the same objectives: for Cuba to be free as soon as possible."

As far as I know, the FBI was not created to fight for the freedom of any other country, nor is this one of its functions. However, these statements clearly highlight the political agenda of the FBI office in south Florida.

Coincidentally, these statements were made in October of 1990, precisely at the beginning of a decade in which terrorist acts against Cuba from south Florida would be stepped up considerably.

Statements like these, coming from an FBI agent and made on a radio station show with the above-mentioned characteristics, could only serve to encourage the organizers of terrorist acts against Cuba and offer them the security that they will not be persecuted for their actions.

Mr. Héctor Pesquera, the agent in charge of the south Florida FBI office, appeared as a guest on the same station, the same show, and with the same host, just days after the verdict was announced in our trial.

In the face of these realities, what can Cuba do to defend itself and be forewarned of terrorist plans?

Can the authorities of the south Florida FBI be trusted when it comes to matters related to Cuba's national security?

Can someone who is here to look into the activities of terrorist groups and to prevent their actions in order to deter the death of innocent people be officially registered with the U.S. government?

What can Cuba do to defend its people, when boats leaving Florida loaded with weapons to attack Cuba are seized by the U.S. authorities, and those authorities are satisfied with explanations like, "We're lobster fishing"? We heard this in this very courtroom from an ATF agent who intercepted a boat loaded with weapons and maps of Cuba just 40 miles off its coasts.

On July 23, 1998, the *Miami Herald* reported comments made by terrorist Tony Bryant, who laughed over how he was questioned by FBI officials after his boat was found near Havana with explosives on board. According to what Bryant told the newspaper, he promised he would not do it again, and they let him go.

What can Cuba do when terrorists like Virgilio Paz and José Dionisio Suárez, who blew Orlando Letelier and Ronnie Moffit to bits in this country's capital and were then fugitives from the law, serve only seven years of their sentences and are then back on the streets thanks to the assistance of the CANF, which paid for their legal defense? I know of cases of reentry that have been given longer sentences than that.

The first words spoken to the press by one of these two individuals were to thank the CANF, Armando Pérez Roura and WAQI for the efforts they had made to get both of them released. This is the same radio station and the same radio show host for whom FBI agents Berlingueri and Pesquera appeared as guests.

The truth is that Cuba has no choice but to have people here, acting out of love for their country, and not for money, to keep the country informed of terrorist plans and to keep those plans from execution whenever possible. That is the reason for my presence here.

As long as the situation remains as I have described it, Cuba has a moral right to defend itself in the way that my comrades and I have done it.

Your Honor:

On September 11, we were all witnesses to a horrific and criminal act. An ephemeral act which dismayed the majority of the world's inhabitants, who learned of these events through the television networks. The terrorist acts committed against Cuba for years have not been broadcast by any of those networks.

Allow me to recall that also on September 11, but in 1980, Félix García, a Cuban diplomat accredited to the United Nations, was murdered in New York City by one of the terrorists currently imprisoned alongside Posada Carriles in Panamá.

In the outcome of the terrorist acts that took place in New York and Washington, the world's awareness of the need to eradicate terrorism has increased.

Barely hours, or even minutes, after these events, all of the analysts and high-level officials of this country's government were offering statements, information and viewpoints through the media. They all emphasized the need to speed up intelligence work and to infiltrate the groups that perpetrate such acts, as well as those who give them support and shelter.

I am convinced that the United States would feel proud of any one of its sons who had the opportunity and the privilege to prevent acts like the ones that took place this past September. Anyone who achieved this would have done a great service to his country and to humankind.

President Bush, in his speech to the joint session of the Congress on September 20, 2001, declared:

"Tonight, we are a country awakened to danger and called to defend freedom."

Your Honor:

My country and my people were forced to awaken to danger and called to defend freedom over 40 years ago. I feel proud to have been one of those who forewarned my people of such dangers.

Later that night, in that same speech, President Bush stated:

"We will come together to strengthen our intelligence capabilities, to know the plans of terrorists before they act and to find them before they strike."

Cuba, which has suffered terrorist attacks for 42 years, also has the right to defend itself in this way. Today, the American nation has joined in the fight against terrorism, something that has been a necessity and a reality for my country for many years.

There can be no double standards. Terrorism must be combated and eliminated whether it is committed against a big and powerful country or against small countries. There is no such thing as bad terrorism and good terrorism.

In the report on Orlando Bosh submitted in 1989 by Undersecretary of Justice Joe D. Whitley, whose administrative position made him less subject to political pressures or foreign policy considerations, this U.S. government official stated:

"The United States cannot tolerate the inherent inhumanity of terrorism as a way of settling disputes. Appeasement of those who would use force will only breed more terrorists. We must look on terrorism as a universal evil, even if it is directed toward those with whom we have no political sympathy."

Your Honor:

Today, you will conclude this stage of our trial and pronounce the sentence that you deem appropriate.

Finally, I simply want to reiterate that at no time did I endanger the national security of the United States, nor was this ever my intent, or that of my comrades.

What I did was inspired by love for my country, and by the conviction that history will register that this is the only choice left to the Cuban people to prevent the death of innocent people and the destruction wrought by the terrorist acts committed against my country.

It is up to the U.S. government to bring an end to these acts. Cuba has shown its willingness to cooperate with the U.S. authorities in this and other areas, like drug trafficking. This would serve the best interests of both nations, since it does affect the national security of the United States.

It is the authorities of this country that must decide to act on the basis of principles, and to shake off the destructive influence of a small but economically powerful group of mobsters and ultra-right fanatics from the Cuban community in Miami.

I sincerely trust that one day Cuba will have no need for people like me to come to this country, voluntarily and out of love for their country and their people, to fight against terrorism.

The first duty of any self-respecting person is to his or her country. Throughout the years of my imprisonment, I will always carry with me the dignity I have learned from my people and their history.

Thank you very much.

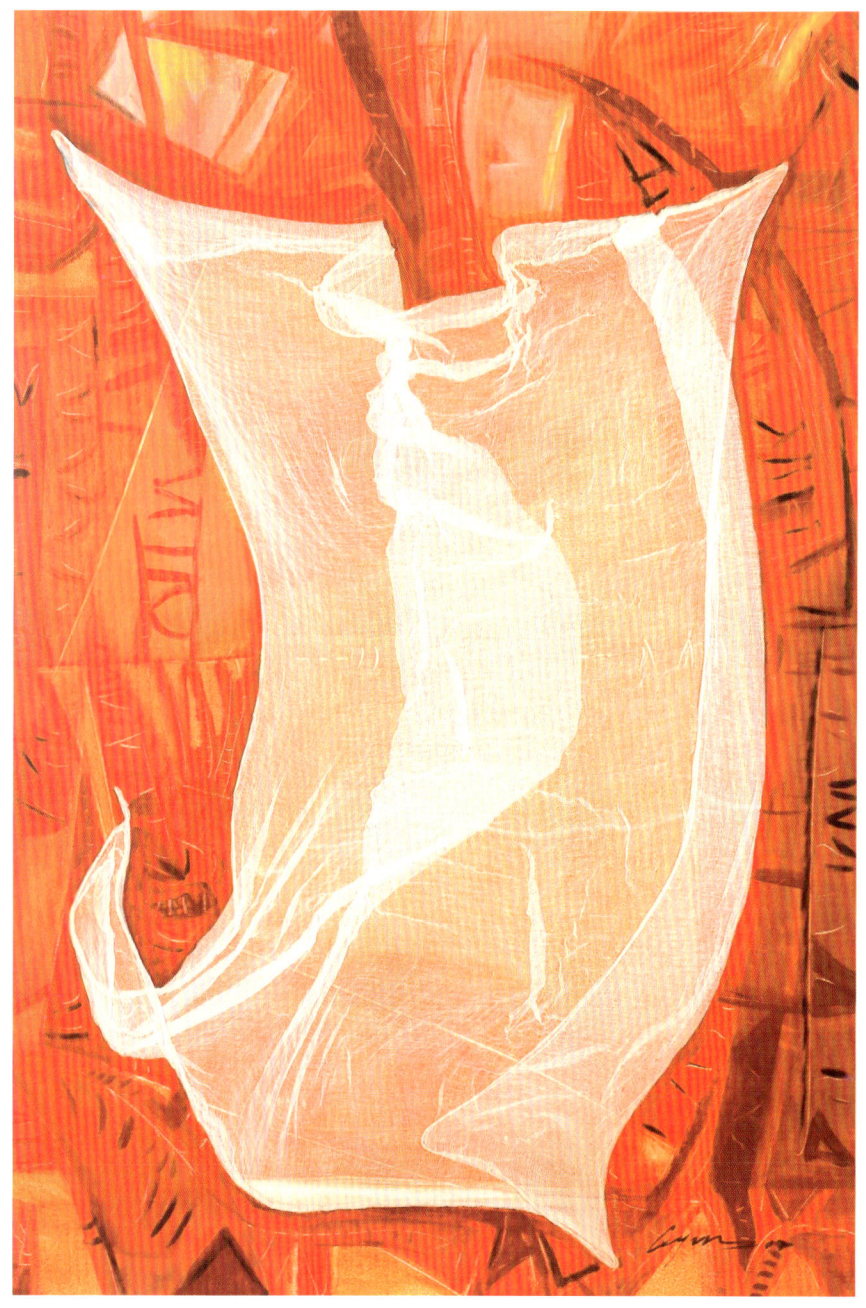

For Freedom   Esteban Leyva

Five years after our court statements

It'll be five years next December 2006 since the presentation of our Court statements, minutes before the Miami Federal Court passed sentence.

Those were intensive days for the Five, very emotional, and full of political and moral significance.

A few months before, a Jury made up by twelve Miami residents had made an extremely unfair decision and declared us all guilty of each and every one of the accusations brought against us by the US administration through its prosecutors. However, during the six-months trial we had proven the hypocrisy of the authorities that raised the accusations and their defense of the Cuban-American terrorists; how they covered up these individuals' long history of terrorist actions against our country and Cuba's necessity to have people like us in South Florida to obtain information on their plans to carry out violent actions against our country. This peaceful work was only intended to save the lives of both Cubans and Americans.

During the trial preceding the sentence hearings held in December 2001, with the support of our attorneys and through the evidence introduced by them and the statements of witnesses, a resounding denunciation was made and demolishing blows dealt to the case constructed by the prosecution against us.

The hysteria of the Cuban-American Mafia in Miami reflected in the press reports and op-eds published in the final days of the trial by the local newspapers they control is ample evidence of this. They showed the impact of the denunciation and the exposure of the true culprits who should have been sitting on the dock instead of us, that is, the criminals of Cuban descent living in the United States and operating from its territory.

After a few months and the outrageous and unjust guilty verdict issued by a Jury which did not ask a simple question or requested a clarification despite the length of the trial, the high number of witnesses and the technical complexity of some issues, the time had come to receive our sentences.

Our people had been informed of the case and knew of the absurd verdict issued against us by a Jury that was not unbiased, nor could it be.

Our people, for many years the victim of terrorist actions organized and financed with impunity in the US territory, and aware of the direct or indirect complicity in those actions of the same authorities that brought us to trial, with its natural sensitivity showed its indignation by unleashing a massive movement of denunciation of the false accusations that would lead to our condemnation and a public campaign of solidarity aimed at attaining justice for us.

The response of the US authorities once again exhibited its hatred and its thirst for revenge: they sent us back to the punishment cells.

When the moment came to hear our sentences it was a matter of honor and dignity to us to expose the Court to the truth. We responded to the slanders of the prosecutors, who had constructed a case against us, by clearly explaining to the members of the Jury the prejudices against Cuba and the Revolution that so many years of disinformation and obsolete propaganda have brought to bear on the Miami community. That had been the prosecution strategy and that's why they fervently opposed, as they still do, holding the trial outside this city.

There were other factors in those days that influenced the proceedings. Five men arrested with us on September 1998 had yielded to pressures of the FBI, which turned them into witnesses of the US administration against us. As of this moment they entered into a spiral of moral and political deterioration in an attempt at justifying their conduct against our people.

We could not forget that we were in the territory of our political adversary, imprisoned by its authorities and accused by prosecutors representing the government whose political elite is bent on the destruction of the Cuban Revolution and the transformation of our country into an economic, political and cultural appendix of the United States of America.

It was then the task of the Five to continue what our attorneys had started during the trial and prove to the political adversaries of our country, to the Cuban Miami Mafia and to the US government that what defines Cuba and its people is its dignity, its honor and its fighting spirit.

These were some of the circumstances that prevailed in those days and in the weeks prior to them; they may help understand the high morale we had at the moment of the sentence hearings when we delivered our Court statements.

Our mothers and some other relatives were sitting in the courtroom during those hearings as well as a representation of the Cuban consulate, which added a more special significance to the situation.

As an offense to our human dignity and honor we were taken to the courtroom, and kept during the hearings, in shackles binding our legs at the ankles. However, this did not prevent us from walking to the podium, albeit with difficulty, to expose from there the truth that had to be heard.

For the first time since our arrest in September 1998, we were personally and publicly denouncing the political nature of the trial and exposing the prosecution and its dirty maneuvers as well as its indiscriminate and opportunistic use of the community prejudices against Cuba to elicit a guilty verdict from the jurors.

There in Miami, before a representation of the Cuban-American Mafia attending the hearings, not only the history of terrorism against Cuba was exposed but also the acquiescent complicity of the authorities that hypocritically accused us and now demanded exorbitant sentences absolutely out of proportion to the crimes of which the jury had unjustly declared us guilty.

It's not difficult to imagine our deep emotion and our sense of responsibility in those hours.

The hypocrisy of the entire process and the political nature of our case grew more evident in those days, at the end of December 2001. Coincidentally, in those same days, the United States government, on behalf of an alleged confrontation with terrorism, responded to the crime of September 11 with a ruthless campaign of bombing on Afghanistan. This campaign carried out with the most sophisticated military technology against one of the most backward countries on Earth, took the lives of thousands of innocent civilians.

It's paradoxical and a show of hypocrisy that while the murderous bombs were dropped on the helpless population of Afghanistan, we were sentenced in a Miami Federal Court to long sentences for trying to prevent terrorist actions, having done so peaceably, never using any weapons or endangering the life of a human being. The US government could use the destructive power of its weapons and take the lives of thousands of innocents on behalf of an alleged war on terrorism, which rather seemed an act of vengeance. Yet, for that government, Cuba, that has been the target of attacks for more than four decades, has no right to peacefully obtain information on terrorist plans hatched against it from US territory, under the very nose of its authorities that would do nothing to prevent it.

This is the truth, and such is the hypocrisy and double standard applied by the US government. This is the political nature of our case. And it is in such circumstances that we were given our sentences and that we made our statements in court.

It was very clear that we were condemned and sentenced not because we had committed a crime but because we are Cuban revolutionaries.

The entire process was designed to please the Cuban Miami Mafia as the first to be informed by the FBI of our arrest were the representatives of that Mafia in the US Congress; the political nature of the case was thus evidenced.

It is a known fact how we were treated after this: seventeen months of isolation in punishment cells from which we were taken out only after filing demands through our defense attorneys.

Today, five years later, as I reread our Court statements I can only reaffirm what every one of us said before receiving our sentences. Our arguments are as valid today as they were back then. The time passed since December 2001, the developments that followed and the information that has come to light in this period confirm what we said in those, for us, significant days.

We would later learn from public statements by Hector Pesquera, chief of the FBI Miami Bureau, that our arrest was made possible by his own personal efforts with the Department of Justice, against the opinion of many FBI officers. These efforts he made to please the Cuban Miami Mafia. There is no other explanation.

The Atlantic magazine , in its November issue this year publishes an extensive report on the cases of Orlando Bosch and Luis Posada Carriles. The article, the result of an over six-month investigation, was written by journalist Ann Louise Bardach who had interviewed Posada Carriles in 1998 and published a series of three articles in *The New York Times* taking after that interview where Posada admitted to have organized the attacks with explosives on hotels in Havana the year before, for which he received funds from the Cuban Miami Mafia.

In this new investigative report, the journalist explains how in 1998 FBI officers in possession of concrete information on Posada Carriles' responsibility with the explosions that damaged hotels in Havana and killed Italian citizen Fabio di Celmo received from their superiors an order to close the case because, for certain groups in Miami, Posada Carriles was a "freedom fighter".

Likewise, the upper echelons denied the FBI officers permission to tap Orlando Bosch's telephone, thus preventing an investigation into this terrorist's criminal plans.

It's a known fact that Orlando Bosch continues to appear in the Miami local television, giving interviews where he publicly advocates the use of violence against Cuba and justifies without remorse the terrorist act against a Cubana de Aviación airliner, which occurred thirty years ago and for which he has not been punished. However, despite all of his statements, the US authorities have not bothered him.

At this point, I should make an indispensable digression. It's true that among my assignments I temporarily took on the surveillance of this terrorist but to honor the truth history should register that Gerardo was responsible for this task and he was the one who devoted most energies and time to its planning, organization and materialization. It was Gerardo who carried out this mission for a long time, and it is only fair to make it known.

Back to the information that keeps coming to light and confirms the arguments contained in our Court statements, the abovementioned articles, based on the journalist's sources in the FBI Miami Bureau, report that officers there had been ordered to close every case related with Cuban-American terrorists' plans and to concentrate on finding Cuban "spies."

The same report brings the information that the FBI Miami Bureau had destroyed the evidence in the Posada Carriles' case, a decision requiring approval not only from the chief of that Bureau but also from the Department of Justice. Bearing in mind Posada Carriles's terrorist history and the political atmosphere following the events of 9/11, the destruction of the evidence in his case must have been a political decision made at the government top levels.

The case of terrorist Luis Posada Carriles, the lenient treatment received by him and his accomplices, and the conspiracy of the United States authorities to finally release the terrorist constitute the epitome of hypocrisy and double standard exercised by the US government on the issue of terrorism when it comes to Cuba. It is also an irrefutable proof of the political nature of our case and of the aberrant sentences we were given.

It also comes to confirms what we said in our Court statements five years ago, that Posada Carriles, during his imprisonment in Panama, received the support of the most prominent members of the Cuban Miami Mafia. Today we also know, as Ann Louise Bardach has revealed, that the three Cuban-American representatives of that Mafia in the US Congress, using stationary with the sign of the United States Congress, wrote a letter to the then President of Panama Mireya Moscoso, to intercede in favor of Posada Carriles and the terrorists who were in prison with him for their release.

These legislators, elected with the money and influence of the Cuban Miami Mafia, protect terrorists; from their official positions in the legislative branch of the US administration, Ileana Ros-Lehtinen, Mario Díaz-Balart and Lincoln Díaz-Balart give protection to anti-Cuban terrorism. The latter took part in a local television program in Miami where he defended the idea of murdering Commander in Chief Fidel Castro. Only in Miami, and about Cuba, could a member of the Federal Congress make such statements advocating the assassination of the Head of State from another country without eliciting any questioning or being forced to abdicate his position or be arrested.

These are just a few of the developments and the information that has come to light, which confirm the veracity and truthfulness of our Court statements and their validity. They also allow for a better understanding about the need for our presence in South Florida.

As I said on December 2001, the dignity we have learned from our people and its history keeps us company, and the truth of our case keeps gaining ground slowly but steadily thanks to the efforts of not only the Cuban people but of hundreds of thousands of friends, too; honest men and women from all over the world.

Five years ago, on December 2001, our Court statements were ignored by a magistrate who decided to give us long prison sentences. Although she heard all of the evidence on the terrorist attacks against Cuba, the Judge could not or did not want to understand the historical reasons of our people's fight nor our position based on dignity and honor.

The irrational sentences given to us turned the Judge into a conscious or unconscious instrument of the Cuban Miami Mafia and the US authorities who are its accomplices.

However, our arguments were heard by those who really count: the men and women from all over the world who are today our companions in this struggle. Together with the Cuban people, they will make those arguments we exposed in our Court statements be heard by other people and all together they will then open the way for justice to be served and for us to return to our Homeland.

Fernando González Llort

They defend our dreams — JOSÉ OMAR TORRES

miguel barnet

so far and yet so near a message to the Five

When Arleen asked me to send you a message telling you something about myself and about Cuba, of course, I couldn't say no but, at the same time, I didn't know what to say. How could I say anything to you who are so far and yet so near? It then occurred to me to write a text that would start by saying that being in jail is hard but that you're free, because freedom is not something you beg for or that you borrow but rather something that you carry inside despite rulings and injustices. Then, as I'm approaching the Radio Rebelde studio, — just before I start climbing the stairs of what in my youth we called CMQ[1], which is today the ICRT[2] — some ideas come to mind and I want to write a situation poem, but writing a situation poem is no easy task, least of all to you, for you know very well what poetry is; you know better than I do because poetry is for you a source of nourishment, a necessity and not a luxury of words or an intellectual exercise. Then, right there, at the ICRT lobby, I wrote these lines which are but a solidarity message; solidarity, yes, a common word that hits me now with its full meaning and lofty value, because overuse can make words loose their meaning that they only recover when they're more than simple words because they are spoken from deep inside our hearts.

And so it happened that in that program in which I told you so much about things that are mine and that are Cuban and so they're yours too, I started saying that being in jail is hard, or rather that I think being in jail is hard, and that others like the Turkish

---

[1] CMQ, name given to the Cuban Radio and Television Agency before 1959.(N.of the T.)
[2] ICRT, by its acronym in Spanish (Instituto Cubano de Radio y Televisión), Cuban Radio and Television Agency. (N. of the T.)

poet Nazim Hiknet and the Salvadoran poet Roque Dalton were in jail too, and that behind the cold and silent iron bars of their prison cells, or rather behind the very cold and very silent iron bars of their prison cells, they still sang Turkish songs and songs from the Spanish Civil War, like that about the Fifth Regiment.

I'm not asking you to sing Turkish songs or songs from the Spanish Civil War because you sing the songs of Miguel Matamoros and Silvio Rodríguez, and you also write situation poems, poems which are like hugs and letters, and like invisible threads, and you read Gramcsi and Fidel who were behind iron bars, too.

Neither am I asking you to fetch me a blue star, for it would be too much to ask. I'm asking nothing from you; I rather want to give you a bit of my voice, just a bit of my humble voice, which is the most I can give you although I would like to have a big medieval door key, one of those enormous medieval keys that open castles and are now in museums although they can also open every prison cell; a master key so that no one gets me wrong because even when at this very moment you are behind bars I know you have not lost your freedom, another common word that now hits me with its full meaning.

Freedom, my brothers, belongs to all those who feel free, and even as you are behind bars in a dark prison cell, you're freer than the wind.

Flight to freedom   EVER FONSECA

laidi fernández de juan

To Fernando González Llort
Who will be back.
To her, who's waiting for you,
And to the poet,
Whose verses I borrowed.

CERTITUDE

DAY 1. Six months have passed since we last met and I think I'm starting to feel relieved. Perhaps today you mean less to me than you did. I think you'll be happy when you know it because if you were ever as much as touched by guilt, this instead of gnawing at you will be more tenuous and it might end up confounded with the puffing breeze.

I'm glad, too. As from today, all the energies I spent on you for many years, and above all in the past few months since the girl selling plastic flowers managed to conquer you, will have another purpose.

Thanks to all things my spirit had to resort to, unfocused as it was due to your neglect, you'll ultimately start on your way to oblivion.

For instance, I'll no longer watch the light of the candles that I've been lighting for you one-hundred-and-eighty days, near the only picture I still have of the two of us. As I read in one of those esoteric books my friends gave me, it's necessary to devote several minutes to watch the lit candles if you really one to guess how the fairies and the angels perceive the possibilities of a return.

It was rather difficult in the first few months until I only had to look at the flame to know the predictions for each day.

Your mind, in the absence of these figments of the imagination that do not belong in the field of rationality, exempts you from understanding the meaning of a shaking flame or a weeping candle, the meaning of the flame being more or less alive or dividing into two or looking like a spiral, or sparkling in the air or burning with a bluish light.

But, my mind, superior to yours in these matters, when it received in the morning the message sent through my eyes that the wick of the candle was lighter than ever, it knew right away that today, after six months of absence, you'll start to fade away, and that's a fact.

It's not chance. I assure you that this bright light today, as well as the dreams visiting me lately, which I interpret according to the dictionary of dreams (another one of the books I consult), the way the sunflowers lean to me today instead of leaning to the sun, the speed at which the bouquets of flowers are withering, the sudden strength of the ferns in the garden and other things of the magic world, are signs that you will start being replaced.

I know very well that your towering vanity leaves no space to concern, that your skepticism will protect you and that until today your lapidary style makes you believe that my soul belongs to you.

And, so it was. When I recall the years I spent all my forces on you, I feel sorry that it's a case of beating a dead horse. However, that sorrow which is a combination of arrogance for the time I wasted and pity for you, because no one will ever love you like this, starts to fade away. Believe me, today you shall walk right into my past (like that *tango* we enjoyed together) even if I don't know myself where I'm going to place the hope I read about in the book on the seven spiritual laws of success, *Las siete leyes espirituales del éxito*.

DAY 2. The expert who reads the Tarot cards wanted to know if I was still interested in his reading since I had made the reservation several weeks ago. I was tempted to say no, that I was fed up with overenthusiastic responses to my questions; that even if at the beginning I found consolation in all the fortune tellers who invoking a gypsy said to me that your return was so imminent that it made their hair stand on end, I could no longer believe.

I wanted to say no, because far from seeing into my future these women had allowed me to discover that I am nobody's daughter; because it doesn't seems serious to me that one assures me in August that I am Xango's daughter, while another in October says that I'm protected from the depth of the Earth by Oya, and still another one in November is certain that Yemaya is my mother.

Then I thought that the Tarot reading didn't have to be any better than all the other sessions where spiritualism, shaped in predictions, would give me instructions that if I observed to the letter would ensure your return (which they promised, anyway).

When a woman has taken a bath whipping her body with star apple leaves after submerging in a bathtub full of daisy flowers and drinking honey with dry wine, without ever obtaining what she so earnestly prayed for, it is only natural that she no longer believes.

I thought about telling all this to the man who reads the Tarot, but I didn't. I did visit him though, but I was as tired and apathetic as he who has seen it all.

The major secrets started to crop up. The best card, the one that shows an enormous sun, fell in the center surrounded by the others. *The man with the name that you have mentioned will return; don't you doubt it.*

That's what the expert said. I smiled at him hiding my lack of faith, and I walked out. I stopped at the Malecon, and sat on the seawall, with my feet hanging over the sea, staring at the fanciful waves. They were in complete disarray, some hiding beneath the others; the former seemed to get upset and the latter intertwined looking for protection. I tried to understand the meaning of this marine indiscipline but then I remembered my determination to stop seeing signals everywhere, and I turned to look away.

There was another woman sitting on the wall, a few feet from me. I went up to her in a sort of female solidarity gesture.

—Is there anything I can do for you? I asked.

—No, thanks, I come often to look at the ocean, she said. My name is Rosa A., and yours?

—Maria E., nice meeting you. Are you waiting for somebody? I wanted to know.

—I am, always. But he is far away, she said.

—That happens. Would you tell me his name?

Then I knew I couldn't help but finding signals everywhere I looked around me. The man Rosa A. is waiting for has the same name as you. They are separate and she is looking at the ocean waiting for an answer. This cannot happen by chance.

DAY 3. Although we didn't make any arrangements we met again. I wanted to get rid of the attributes which had kept me company for months; I was carrying candles, incense and a cobble stone that for no reason I had identified as a likely medium between the heavenly universe and me, and I walked towards the Victor Hugo park.

I had initially thought of throwing everything to the ocean, but it would have been an ecological insult and who knows if, after all, Yemaya is my mother. Then it occurred to me that the garbage can in any corner of the city could be the right place for these objects that had ultimately entertained my illusion with the absurdity of your return; but I found it too rude.

I didn't like any of these options, so I walked to the park where there is this giant cotton tree where pumpkins, black plantains tied with a red ribbon and dead chicken usually show up, mysteriously.

Actually, I wanted to get rid of you and to do that I had to put away any announcement about your return made by the candle flames, the aroma of incense and the cold look of a cobble stone.

Perhaps, even if my intention is that you mean less to me, a very small part of me does not relinquish the possibility that the old hope may return. I needed to give myself some kind of truce at sunset, and there is no better place for that than a cotton tree.

So, I placed all my strange offerings among other objects, including a pineapple surrounded by flies, and I sat on one of the benches in the park around the pergola. Even if I was determined to forget you, and because of that, I was taken over by a feeling of sadness I could not explain. I realized that love wastes and confounds as an unearned fortune.

Some time later Rosa A. arrived. She walked like a Spartan fortress; it was impressive. After sitting on the bench nearest to mine, she started reading from a bundle of letters tied with a blue ribbon.

It was a very old image, but she didn't mind being ridiculous. Perhaps she knew that solitude is, above all, shameless. As you know I believe in chance. I know that life loves theatricals so I came up to her and reminded who I was. She looked at me annoyed for I had interrupted her reading, but it was a qualified annoyance, like that of angels.

Day 4. The pragmatism of Rosa A. is amazing.

I explained to her that according to some Oriental theories, every difficulty in life is but a challenge that should make us stronger (I read it in one of those books I mentioned before). I said that we should find power in the flowers, in the mirrors and in prayers. She interrupted me categorically saying that one doesn't pray to God, but demand from God.

I must admit that I was overcome by emotion. We exchanged our stories with that bizarre complicity that grows between strangers only to discover that we had married the same year, that we have been alone the same time, and that our men like the same beer and the same music, and that both are good readers.

That is, you and he have many things in common, in addition to women who are getting to know each other. Unlike me —I'm terrified of being anonymous— Rosa

A. only speaks the indispensable. It struck me that she was so calmed while she told me her story while I'm always so very anxious.

I told her about your new woman, who sells plastic flowers. I told her how you and I laughed at her frivolity, her hairstyle, the excess of makeup on her face every time we walked into her shop, and I confessed that I would have never thought that one day you would live with such a person.

When I was finished, Rosa A. said nothing like that had happened to her, that although our stories coincided in dates and I was bent on finding you, I had lost you, just like things are lost in the sea.

At this point in our conversation it was obvious that our differences would prevent another encounter. I said that it had been a pleasure to meet her and that I wished her all the luck in the world; time would say which of the two men, with the same name, would return first.

She almost smiled, and it was like a crystal smile, and she said good-bye with these words that could not be more bizarre:

—You still don't get it, do you? All your predictions, your prayers, your astral chart, everything has told you the name of he who will return. That's the secret of my peace of mind which bothers you so much. I know who it will be because unlike you, I have never felt his absence. I feel that we share our solitude.

Each one of us took a different way. Just when I crossed the street to go home there was a thunder storm. Now, I'm writing to you without the time or the wishes to know the meaning of that roaring coming from the sky.

This will be the last time. Please, never come back. My lack of faith deserves the punishment of loosing you, and the certitude that the other Fernando will return.

In the wee hours of morning, January 17, 2007

cintio vitier

fernando

Dedicating The sun of the moral world

Luz's words of light to Sanguily
came, shaking like a testament,
in silence to you.

You had to be who you are. The sun
illuminating your inmate's suit
never abandons the honores chest.

I give you my book as the award
you gave me when I asked.
How I long to deserve it this time.

No tittle   JUAN MOREIRA

THE INCARCERATION OF MR. ANTONIO GUERRERO RODRÍGUEZ, MR. FERNANDO GONZÁLEZ LLORT, MR. GERARDO HERNÁNDEZ NORDELO, MR. RAMÓN LABAÑINO SALAZAR AND MR. RENÉ GONZÁLEZ SEHWERERT IS ARBITRARY, AND IT CONTRADICTS ARTICLE 14 OF THE INTERNATIONAL CONVENTION ON CIVIL AND POLITICAL RIGHTS.

Having proclaimed this view, the Working Group appeals to the United States Government to adopt the necessary measures to remedy this situation, in compliance with the principles expressed in the International Convention on Civil and Political Rights.

United Nations Human Rights Commission Working Group on Arbitrary Detentions May 27, 2005

"In our own case, from the ocean of lies in which justice sank, a testimony emerged from a witness who was supposed to identify in a recording the voice of one of the pilots from Brothers to the Rescue who, according to the rest of the evidence, it was impossible to have talked at that time because…
HE WAS ALREADY DEAD!

The shameless explanation of the Prosecution in the face of such absurdity was that "Well, Your Honor, the Jury is free to believe what it chooses."

Another example comes to my mind in our case: the Prosecution wanted to blame me for a letter I had simply not written, and according to the FBI lab tests, the printing did not match my computer's. But that was of no consequence. The gentleman simply stood up in front of the Jury and gave it this message:

"The FBI evidence says one thing but I am the Prosecution and I say a different thing."

THAT GUY HAD ABSOLUTE CERTAINTY THAT HIS ONLY WORD WOULD OVERRIDE NO LESS THAN AN FBI TEST.

René González Sehwerert

May you always have confidence in our victory, and keep up that enthusiasm that I sense in your letter. Let these words bring you all the affection and love of this son who takes pride in your courage and strength in these difficult times...

Excerpts of the first manuscript letter his mother received on February 4, 2001, after several years without exchanging correspondence.

My dear niece:
I believe you when you say that if your maturity depended on this situation you'd rather go on being a baby […] this shows the affection you feel for me and how painful this whole situation is for you […] as you rightly say, at the end of the day you'll be a stronger and more mature Laura. Of course, I'd rather not have you go through this and allow your maturity to come to you less dramatically […]
Receive a very big kiss from your uncle, who loves you very much,

Fernando

There is this close-up of you taken by Bill; it hurts me to part with it, but after months hanging on the mural in my cell I want you to have it and keep it. Because of its size it doesn't fit in my album and I wouldn't like to lose it in one of these transfers to 'the hole'. I part with this picture with the same feeling I part from you at the end of our few visits. It has kept me company in the cell for months. From any angle that I looked at it, it was as if your eyes kept following me. Quite often in my solitude I found myself looking at that picture in an imaginary dialogue with you.

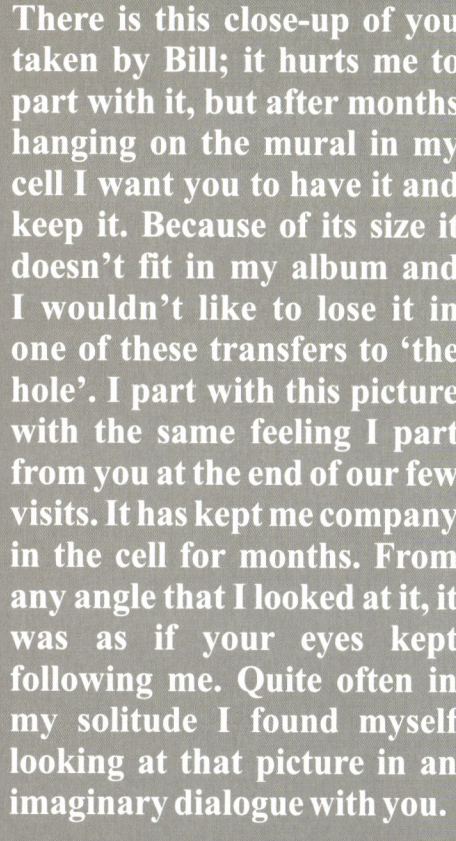

These years in American prisons have forced us to assimilate the reality of the circumstances and to accept it as part of the necessary sacrifice. Still, it's a very painful reality. It is our profound revolutionary conscience, our deepest conviction that truth is on our side and the certainty that we defend a just cause that allows us to put that pain into perspective, to accept reality and to live with it.

However, one of the most painful features of that reality is the children that we would have, that were part of our family plans, the same plans that time has changed into the children that will never be. With the passing of years and the advance of the biological clock, this forced separation leads us to change the vision of our family into a childless family, albeit with much love.

Surely, mine is not the only case. But, what makes our pain special is that this situation and this reality are caused by an enormous injustice…

To Rose
(Excerpt of a letter to his wife) Oxford, Wisconsin

My love:
…I'll rather not mention your health and that you should see the doctor about it as I've already told you on the phone. I'm waiting for the letter where you shall explain about it, but I do want to say —as we have discussed— that whatever the result of the tests and the possibilities to realize our plans, I will continue to love you and want you as no one else in my life.

Rosa:

I don't mind the time we need to wait or the effects of time on us physically. When the time comes for us to meet again, I'll be there with you, so that you don't need to miss me anymore, neither in the morning or the evening. I'll be there in the morning to tell you how well you look in your work uniform, and I'll be there in the evening to repeat it. Then, all this time will be behind us as a distant memory and we shall tell each other stories watching the ocean and holding hands.

My love:

...On the book *Armas, germenes y acero*, published in Cuba by the Science & Technique Publishing House, I remind you to try to get it and read it if you can. I think that scientifically the book is very good. It recounts history from the time man appeared on Earth seven million years ago until the discovery, the conquest and colonization of the New World leading to the reasons that ultimately gave Europe in 1492 the advantage over the rest of the world to advance on the geographic areas it colonized.

...I think you should read the book to follow the logic of this historical process as the author presents it in all detail.

To me, the book's flaw lies in that it fails to offer the concept of the class society; it would only need the addition of this…

...It does not admit that for a long time technology and the knowledge accumulated by humanity would allow a comfortable and dignified life to the inhabitants of the world and that there is no reason for the big differences between the rich and the poor, or between the rich countries and the poor countries. He fails to see that even if until 1492 the development of anthropology and natural sciences in general allowed to explain the influence of geography and the environment on the differences in the evolution and development of the different continents, after the conquest and colonization a system of domination was rooted that not only perpetuates such differences but it deepens them, and that system persists until today…

Today, after three years in prison and about to be sentenced, and after going through the situations you know about, I will not reiterate what I have already said in this letter, but rather use Silvio Rodriguez's phrase in that song that has such a special meaning to us:

I SHALL DIE AS I HAVE LIVED!

Excerpt from a letter Fernando addressed to Rosa Aurora when they were taken to "the hole" for the second time

The Court is urged to remind the witnesses of their right to take the Fifth Amendment to prevent the discussion of terrorist activities against Cuba.

Official documents of the trial. Prosecution's motion, March 20, 2001

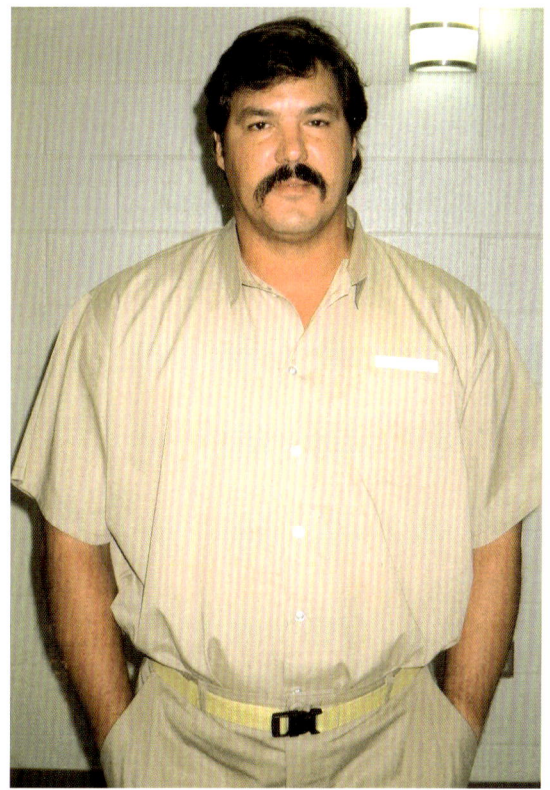

I will wear the prison uniform with the same
honor and pride with which a soldier wears
his most prized insignia.

RAMÓN

marilyn bobes

> *My love, I'll be back to you*
> *In a different morning full of music and poetry,*
> *I'll be back from the Sun that shines on the sweet abyss*
>
> Silvio Rodríguez

A DIFFERENT MORNING FOR RAMÓN

Anette Perdomo had to write an article for her diploma; she was on the point of graduating from journalism. She could freely choose any subject and, in fact, she had in mind the Nueva Trova when she came across a photo of Ramón Labañino. She had mistakenly bought the book bringing the picture for she thought it was about Silvio Rodríguez. It was entitled *Sweet abyss* and in the picture Ramón was standing, his body half-covered in the group he made up with his wife and three daughters. His tender but resolute expression reminded the girl of her dead father killed two years before in a traffic accident.

Anette had closely followed the trial in the United States against that man, and also against Antonio Guerrero, Gerardo Hernández, Fernando González Llort and René González. She had seen their faces many times on television, posters and papers denouncing their situation. But it was only now that Ramón's expression had conjured up a special sentiment. It was the first time she saw him with his family, and she thought nobody had any right to separate him for life from his natural surroundings.

Anette knew that many Cubans living in Miami could be pretty intolerant. She had heard the stories from her cousin Jordanka who had been to Florida in the nineties to visit her sister Danay. According to Jordanka, one night as she was sitting with Danay in the Versalles restaurant waiting to order their meal, a very handsome man in his forties came to their table and asked if he could sit with them.

They agreed, encouraged by his looks, but then he started questioning the visiting girl.

"How long have you been in Miami?" he asked. "Just a few days, but I'm not staying. I'm going back to Cuba in one or two months," she answered.

Her cousin said that the man was so incensed that it was almost irrational. "So, you're a communist, damn it!" he yelled as he grabbed the table to turn it upside down. Everyone there saw it all happen, but no one moved. At that moment Danay, who had lived in Miami long enough to understand what was going on, assured the man that it was all a joke.

"She's lived here since the eighties. She came from Mariel, but she married a French man and lived in Europe sometime after that. Now she's divorced and back for good."

It was only after this explanation that the man changed his attitude and relaxed but Danay was still scared so she got rid of him. She asked him very politely to leave the table because she and her sister were waiting for some friends who would be arriving soon.

Anette was familiar with that face of Miami thanks to this and other stories Jordanka had told her, even if she had some friends there that she believed would never do something like that. On the other hand, she was not surprised that the trial of the five men accused of spying was tainted by prejudice, resentment and bias.

Yet, Anette was doubtful on whether or not to follow this impulse to take up Ramón Labañino's case as the subject of her diploma. She didn't want to write just one more article for, above all, she preferred critical journalism. She was certainly afraid of epic narrative because indiscriminate repetition of certain words commonly used for praising could render them ineffective. But, was this an epic subject? Well, it was, in a way. But it was also a humane subject for it dealt with somebody condemned by the powerful to an undeserved punishment, only for being loyal to his beliefs.

On the other hand, Anette was very curious; she wanted to know who was really this man with that expression on his face that so resembled her father's. But, to be useful her article had to elicit in the readers the particular feelings stirred by Silvio Rodríguez with that beautiful song from which this book derived its title. Could an unassuming student of journalism live up to such high standards?

2

So far, Anette had learned that Ramón had arrived in Miami in the late 1990s, that he had married Elizabeth Palmeiro on June 2, 1990, and that their first daughter, Laurita, was born in 1992. Ramón had by then another daughter from a previous marriage, Ailí; and later he and Elizabeth would have another girl, Lizbeth, conceived when he was already in Miami, in one of those trips he sporadically made to Cuba.

Thus, she estimated that when Labañino left he must have been in his thirties. He had been born in Havana, on June 9, 1963.

Anette found it very moving that this young man had left behind his family, his past as a University students' leader and his *suma cum laude* degree in Economics just to help others. Would she have been capable of doing that? She wasn't sure, especially when this talented economist would work in Miami as a drugstore messenger and a shoe salesman. Obviously, he considered the mission assigned to him high above everything else.

Those who knew Ramón described him as a caring, sociable man who enjoys music, mostly Silvio Rodríguez' and Pablo Milanés' songs, like his wife. He also loves sports, theater and movies and he loves his family, his country and his small everyday world as it shows in the poems and personal letters given to her by the person who would tutor her thesis, no other than Marta Rojas, the well-known journalist and author of four novels that she admires so much.

About 5:30 am, on September 12, 1998, FBI agents knocked on the door of Ramón Labañino whom they took to Headquaters for a "persuasion" interview. According to Marta, they wanted him to betray his mission and to cooperate with them in exchange for some promises.

But there was something that Anette would want to emphasize in her article, and it was Ramón's determination. He would never do like that man he always had suspected, the one with the face of a coward. The document written by Labañino had been given to Anette by a friend from the Capitán San Luis Publishing House who she had approached for help.

The article was entitled "The mirror of his soul", and it read as follows: "He had the face of a chicken, he always did. I had warned against him many times over: a man with the face of a chicken can only be a coward, or worse."

Anette felt she had come across some new information, that is, Ramón's impressions on a traitor whose name was not mentioned but whom he had detected from the first time they met.

The day Ramón was arrested, as he walked handcuffed into the white, cold room, he saw the man's face distorted by fear, on the verge of tears. "I already knew what could be expected of that look, of that chicken face," he said.

As days passed, Ramón learned that the man and some others would cooperate with the United States government and give testimony against him and his four brothers, as he would henceforth call the other four men.

He said that was the hardest part of the whole process, at least what hurt him most. "Despite everything I couldn't believe that someone would do anything like that."

As far a Ramón was concerned, all the "persuasion" efforts failed, therefore, he was taken, together with the other four who refused to become traitors, to the Miami Federal Detention Center, in the very heart of downtown. From the car they were taken straight up to the 13th floor, where they spent 18 days. In the first few days they were denied their right to wash up, to take a shower and even to comb their hair.

Then they were kept for seventeen months in "the hole", as the inmates call a maximum security cell for the extremely dangerous.

According to a description by Gerardo Hernandez published on Bohemia magazine on August 2001, which Anette had found in the library, what the inmates call 'the hole' are very small prison cells with a toilet, a metal sink and a shower; a sort of cement table and chair, and an iron-barred cage. It was in that cell that they had to spend 24 hours. Once a day they were taken out for the so-called 'recreation', but never during weekends or if it rained. Recreation consisted of transferring them to a larger cell with a metal grid for a roof to let the outside air in. The only thing they could do there was walking or jogging.

The trial would be held only two years later. The man whom Ramón had always considered a chicken would testify against the Five.

"There he was, only a few steps away from us, but this time he deceived no one. All the mystic and the justifications were now far behind, there was nothing left of that college intellectual, of that weak and submissive personality, now it was truly him, that shaky, hesitant coward, emboldened by his own sin in front of the prison guards, and of his FBI masters and the government that promised him a mild sentence and the fortune of spending the rest of his life hiding from humanity for fear that his own partners will one day punish him, or worse still, that they consider him useless."

At that moment, the man with the face of a coward committed his last and worst act of cowardice; he became a traitor.

"It was a harsh and painful way to confirm that I had been right after all." Anette thought then that Ramón Labañino Salazar would suffer every injustice in the world but he'd never be a miserable traitor like that pitiful individual.

3

The Judge refused to move the trial to Fort Laudardale, and Anette thought that the fate of the defendants was so decided. As her cousin Jordanka had said, Miami could not be impartial.

The rest was widely known; it was in practically every newspaper. The trial had lasted almost seven months. The defense attorneys called about seventy witnesses including a General, an Admiral and a presidential advisor, and every one of them testified that the defendants had not breached any law of the United States.

In one of the leaflets received from his friend of the Publishing House (The Five: An Untold Story) Anette had underlined three questions that she felt were the key to prove that these Cubans were not guilty. A defense attorney had posed these questions to US Division General Edward Atkenson.

Defense Attorney: "As you reviewed all the materials, did you find any instructions ordering these people to obtain classified documents?"

General Atkenson: "No, I did not."

Defense Attorney: "Did you ever find specific instructions to them to obtain very secret documents?"

General Atkenson: "No, I did not."

Defense Attorney: "Did you ever find any instructions to the agents aimed at obtaining materials harmful to the United States?"

General Atkenson: "No, I did not."

The defense counselors obtained from the same source precise testimony indicating that José Basulto and Rodolfo Frómeta, witnesses for the Prosecution, had admitted in their testimonies having executed terrorist actions against Cuba in the past, and the present. It was then obvious that the five defendants had a moral right to be in Miami to defend their fellow countrymen, targets and victims of those proven and other unproven actions.

Anette remembered those days in 1997 when several Cuban hotels were the targets of such actions, and she also recalled the death of a young Italian, Fabio di Celmo. That same day she had accompanied some Spanish friends to the Capri Hotel, where a bomb had exploded a few hours later. Fortunately, Anette's friends had not been hurt, so they said to her over the phone and now Anette thought that it was perhaps thanks to one of the Five that the Cuban authorities were able to catch the Salvadoran citizen directly involved in the crime, the same that would later confess who the true culprits were.

Despite all this the Cubans had been found guilty of the 26 charges brought up against them. Ramón Labañino would have to serve a life sentence plus 18 more years of imprisonment.

4

In Havana, on June 2001, Elizabeth Palmeiro, still convalescing from surgery, asked her daughter Laurita to come lie down with her for a while; then and there she explained to the girl that her father Ramón was in prison in Miami from September 1998. Anette had read Elizabeth's words in *Sweet Abyss*, the book she had bought when she thought of writing the article on the Nueva Trova.

"I said to her that he was accused of being a spy who had endangered the security of the United States but that it wasn't true, that her father was in prison because he was a good patriot defending the Cuban people from terrorist attacks, and that he had hurt no one. I said that her father was in prison because he had defended us all from death. I also explained that he had been tried in Miami and that they wanted to give him a life sentence."

Laurita burst into tears; only Ramón's letters, which started coming at the end of December 2000, could begin to fill up the emptiness they felt.

December 2000
FDC-Miami

"My loving wife, dearest family:

"After a "long" period of silence, I take advantage of this opportunity to tell you how much I love every one of you, and how I yearn to see you all again (…)

"(…) You can't imagine how I yearn for the day when I can hear your voice and the girls'; it will be like a "dream" (…)

"As for the rest, don't you worry for everything will come up to light and "the truth will make us free", like an all-time genius has said.

"Papo, papi."

4

Some time after their sentences were pronounced, the Five were transferred to different prisons in various states, after another inhumane stay in "the hole". Ramón Labañino is still held in the same prison located at Beaumont, Texas, which was inaugurated as a maximum, medium and minimum security prison en 1966. The number of inmates there exceeds its capacity. It's a place where fist-fights and violence prevail and gang members kill each other, which causes the so-called lockdowns of all the penal population.

That kind of disciplinary measure, which is rather common in Beaumont, affects family visits, personal hygiene as well as the possibility to make telephone calls. Ramón lives in danger of being murdered o assaulted due to the existing hostility in the place where he has been taken with all sorts of delinquents and criminals. Additionally, he is subjected to a special security regime that demands that he registers with the prison authorities every two hours.

Anette read in a Juventud Rebelde newspaper special supplement, from which she extracted that information, that in prison Ramón works as a janitor in the laundry room and the rest of his time he uses to exercise, read and respond the great number of letters he receives under the name of Luis Medina, No.58734-004, USP Beaumont, PO BOX 26035, Texas 77720-6035 USA. One day she will perhaps forward him her article or write him a letter.

It was precisely in that prison, and before that in another prison in Miami, that Ramón Labañino wrote the poems published in Holguín under the title "White Seagulls". Anette had spent the night reading these poems. They were not the work of a skillful poet but they expressed the deep sentiments of a human being whose need for communication lead him to use a moving language he is not familiar with but is impregnated with his essence; a language that in Ramón's case is not only soft and clear but also rebellious.

Here I am, amidst scoundrels and detritus,
Between dawns that never happen and
A swarm of nightmares, of nightmares (…)

What Ramón said in his poem was that "I fight sufferings and promises/the nightmarish hours of solitude/the threat of drugs and violence."

The next day, as Anette continued her readings, she learned more about the Court in Atlanta. The defense attorneys had filed an appeal with the 11th Circuit Court of Appeals in that city.

On August 9, 2005, three judges annulled the Miami trial. For a moment tensions eased and hopes cropped up, but it would be only for a year, because on August 9, 2006, a full panel of judges from the same Court, by a majority vote, repealed the previous three-judge decision and denied the possibility of a new trial.

Anette thought of the terrible blow that the refusal to revoke the sentences had meant, both for the prisoners and their families. She then recalled the day when a police agent had come to her house to report her father's death. She re-lived that pain and felt that Elizabeth, Ramón and his three daughters must have gone through a similar experience.

But Ramón Labañino and his comrades were not dead like her father. They were alive, and while there is life, there is hope.

Again, Anette felt that she must follow her impulse. Her subject for the diploma dissertation could be no other than the case of Ramón Labañino, the man with the same tender but resolute expression of her father. Anette felt a pressing need to do it.

5

Urgent norks was the way Mario Benedetti defined that literature where, because of its significance, content takes precedence over form. Anette had before her eyes the notes that could help her compose a sort of puzzle whose parts were all dispersed waiting for somebody to put them together properly. She realized that writing the article she could contribute, however modestly, to denounce a cruel injustice, but she still feared that her text would not live up to the expectations.

On her working table she had all the information she had collected. A story of which she had known only pieces before came up now as a sordid chronology of abuses. That story had to be recounted once again, even if it seemed that everything had already been said. Maybe her article would not be published in the most important newspapers of the world. As a matter of fact, very few people outside Cuba and Miami were familiar with these events.

Perhaps, not even Granma would publish it for she was no more than a student of journalism who had found a subject for her diploma. Yet, she would write it. She didn't mind where it was published; she needed to strive, at least with words, against that ruling dictated by hatred.

Suddenly she wished above all else to have the talent to be a writer. If she could at least produce literature…

She imagined a story of which she knew only the ending. At the end of this story Ramón set foot on Cuban soil after traveling on a plane very much like the one that brought Elián González back home. She could see the shining face of Elizabeth Palmeiro, and the clear, innocent smiles of Ailí, Lizbeth and Laurita. It would all happen one morning, a different morning full of music and poetry. She knew that only so often fiction became a reality. It would suffice if many were touched by this story.

Ramón Labañino and the others deserved that happy ending and it would be theirs not in literature but in real life, because they were not alone.

American writer Raymond Carver said that "words, precise and real words" can have the power of actions. Anette agreed with that assertion, that's why she had studied journalism. She needed to find those 'precise and real words'. She had to invent a different morning for Ramón. She had to bring him back from the Sun. She had to tell the world or whoever wanted to listen or had the possibility to listen that there was a man waiting for himself "far, far away, climbing the sweet abyss."

She would write that article, she definitely would; she would write it and rewrite it until she found the precise words, until she was exhausted.

We are all The Five   ALEXIS LEYVA MACHADO (KCHO)

Defense statement presented by Ramón Labañino Salazar at the sentencing hearing held thursday, december 13, 2001

Your Honor, Ladies and Gentlemen:

First of all, I join in all of the arguments put forward by my four brothers in this case and in my recognition of the professional behavior of the officials in this court: Richard, the translators, the marshals, and Lisa.

The criminal attacks on the Twin Towers in New York and the Pentagon in Washington took the lives of thousands of innocent people in the United States, and we share in the anger and sorrow of the American people. It is our fervent hope that events like these are never repeated.

We who have devoted our lives to fighting terrorism, to preventing atrocious acts like these from taking place; we who have tried to save the lives of innocent human beings not only in Cuba but in the United States as well, stand in this courtroom today to be sentenced precisely for preventing similar acts. Thus, this punishment could not be more ironic and unfair!.

The words of George W. Bush, president of this country, in the name of which I am to be sentenced, clearly express the reasons why we came to the United States and why we find ourselves in this courtroom today.

From this very city of Miami, terrorist acts against my country, Cuba, have been planned, organized and directed. From here, the terrorists and their activities are sponsored, encouraged and financed. They are given shelter here as well. To mention just one well-known case, a terrorist and murderer not only of Cubans but of people from the United States as well, Orlando Bosch, freely walks the streets of Miami. And what is most regrettable of all is that all of this takes place with the knowledge and consent of this country's authorities. One need only thoroughly read all of the evidence in our case, which gives a full account of all these kinds of terrorist activities.

Cuba, my country, has suffered more than 42 years of terrorist acts, aggression, invasions and provocations, which have resulted in the deaths of over 3478 innocent human beings and physical injuries to over 2099. Cuba, like the United States, has the right to defend itself.

To offer just a few examples:

–On March 4, 1960, the French ship *La Coubre* was blown up in the port of Havana by agents of the CIA; 101 people were killed as a result of this terrorist sabotage, including six French sailors.

–On October 6, 1976, in a treacherous terrorist attack perpetrated by Luis Posada Carriles and Orlando Bosch, through Venezuelan mercenaries, two bombs were detonated on a Cubana Airlines civilian aircraft that had taken off from the Barbados, cruelly killing 73 people (57 Cubans, including 24 youths from the Cuban National Fencing Team, 11 young people from Guyana, and five Koreans). Some of these terrorist murderers are in prison today in Panama, and enormous efforts are being made here in Miami to have them set free. Here they are called "patriots" and regarded as symbols; radio stations are raising funds for their defense and possible escape from jail.

–There have been 637 attempts on the life of the president of Cuba, Fidel Castro.

–Bacteriological terrorism aimed at humans, plants and animals has also been used against my country, with a total of 344,203 people affected and 158 dead, of whom 101 were children.

This is not paranoia, these are lives of innocent human beings!

These terrorist groups we were acting against not only carried out these kinds of activities in Cuba, but also here in the United States. This news report, which is totally public and available to everyone, provides a summary of the terrorist acts committed here in Miami, a total of over 68 acts of violence. This article written by journalist Jim Mullin of the Miami New Times on April 20-26, 2000, among many other incidents, reports the following:

–1968 Orlando Bosch fires a bazooka from the MacArthur Causeway against a Polish ship (Miami politicians would later declare an "Orlando Bosch Day" to honor this terrorist).

–1974 Exile leader José Elías de la Torriente is murdered in Coral Gables for the failure of an invasion he was to lead to Cuba.

– 1975 Luciano Nieves is murdered after defending peaceful coexistence with Cuba.
– 1976 Emilio Milán, the news director at WQBA-AM, has his legs blown off by a car bomb after publicly condemning the violence perpetrated by the exile community.
– 1981 A bomb explodes in the Mexican consulate on Brickell Ave., in protest over Mexico's relations with Cuba.
– 1996 A bomb explodes in the Little Havana restaurant Centro Vasco, to protest a scheduled concert by Cuban singer Rosita Fornés.
– 2000 On April 11, outside the home of Elián González' relatives in Miami, radio journalist Scott Piasant of Obregón holds up a T-shirt reading "Send the boy home, it's a father's right", and is physically attacked before the police arrive.

These things did not happen in Cuba. They happened here in the United States, in Miami, in the cities and streets of this country where we all live, where you and your children and families walk every day.

In the 1990s, terrorism, raids and provocations against my country were stepped up, until in 1997 there was a wave of terrorist acts against hotels and other tourism establishments that resulted in the murder of an innocent Italian tourist, Mr. Favio Di Celmo.

How many more deaths of innocent human beings must we witness before this insane and absurd policy towards Cuba is ended?

How many more human lives must be lost before the FBI truly fulfills its duty and arrests the real criminals and terrorists who act against the people of the United States itself?

Could it be that this "fight against terrorism" is pure rhetoric?

No, common sense would say that it is not. And that is precisely why we are here today, because we do not want any of these things to happen, neither in Cuba, nor in the United States, or Miami, or any other part of the world. All that we have done is this: to try to save the lives of innocent human beings, by preventing terrorism and preventing a stupid war.

The same pattern can be observed in all of the Cuban-American terrorists we know. José Basulto was recruited and trained by the CIA and used in its war against my country, and he has kept up the practice of terrorism and provocation up until today, just like the members of such organizations as the Cuban-American National Foundation, Alpha 66, Comandos F-4, the Democratic National Unity Party (PUND), Independent and Democratic Cuba (CID), and the many others referred to in our evidence. These terrorists represent to Cuba what the perpetrators of the horrific acts committed against the United States represent to this country.

Cuba has never trusted these characters, and it never will. Nor should the United States trust them, much less protect them. This is a serious mistake, which could explain in part why events like those of September 11 happen.

My country has suffered from terrorism for more than 42 years. Today the United States is suffering, and if this problem is not eradicated at the root, it could continue to suffer tomorrow. Here in the United States there are more than 800 organizations of a violent nature; this country is the one most vulnerable to these kinds of criminal acts. Terrorism is the true enemy of the national security of the United States. Maintaining a stance of inactivity or indifference, or worse yet, of complicity and concealment of terrorists and terrorism, is the worst crime that can be committed against the national security of this nation; and that is precisely what is happening in this case. Those who protect these groups and individuals are the ones really endangering the national security of the United States.

And that is why, from this forum, I denounce the law enforcement agencies of the United States that have concealed and failed to take action against terrorism and terrorists!

For many years, Cuba has passed information on to various government agencies in the United States, up to the highest level; detailed, documented information, complete with names and conclusive evidence of criminal acts and murders. Our own evidence in this case is a full sampling of that information. And even with all this information in their hands, they have done nothing. There has not been a single arrest, or even a single investigation carried out or underway.

With our arrest, all they have attempted to do is to silence the source of information, to keep serious acts of terrorism like these from disclosure and to hide the truth that so brutally hits us today. Moreover, the FBI has conspired with the terrorists themselves and the extreme right wing in Miami to damage and obstruct any kind of rapprochement and cooperation between our two peoples and governments. Meanwhile, the criminals are happily walking the streets outside here today, laughing at this courtroom. There cannot be a greater offense or stain on these authorities, on the flag presiding this courtroom, and on that coat-of-arms representing the ideal of true justice.

All that Cuba wants is to live in peace and tranquillity. It does not want a war, just as the people of the United States do not want a war. The military leaders of the United States do not want it either, because they know very well that Cuba poses no danger whatsoever to this country. That is why our work has also been aimed at preventing a criminal war, which would only lead to the deaths of innocent people, not only from Cuba, but also from the United States.

At no time have we sought out information that could place the national security of this country in danger. This is pure manipulation, which we will never accept, and a reason for which we decided to come to this trial, in addition to clearly exposing the truth about all of the criminal acts perpetrated from U.S. territory against Cuba and the United States itself.

It is not Cuba that has come to the United States for the purpose of an invasion, aggression, or terrorist acts of all kinds. The reality is the complete opposite, and quite simply, Cuba has the basic right to defend itself. That is all that we have done, without causing harm to anyone or anything.

As long as this criminal policy against my people persists, there will continue to be men like us, as a basic measure of self-defense, just as the United States urgently needs to learn about the inner workings of the terrorist organizations attacking it today. This is a reality that no one can bring to an end.

What the members of the Miami extreme right are really seeking is to create a conflict through some sort of provocation that will result in a U.S. military attack against Cuba. And as I have said, this is not what my people, or my government, or the people of the United States want. General Sheehan's testimony regarding the infiltrations into Cuba by Ramón Saúl Sánchez and his "Democracy" group, revealed that he did not want these elements to provoke a war with Cuba, which could cost the lives of many young men in the U.S. armed forces. Numerous similar points of view were expressed in this courtroom.

As for the prosecution, we have seen a truly shameful and reprehensible behavior that has nothing to do with justice and the search for truth. They first tried to suppress all of our evidence on the terrorist acts perpetrated both in Cuba and here in the United States. They used every means possible to try to suppress 90% of our evidence in this case, that is, the truth about our mission here.

The prosecutors have manipulated and distorted the facts. They have tried to control this courtroom at all times. They have used both subtle and blatant threats. They have resorted to blackmailing witnesses under the threat of legally incriminating them if they did not plead the Fifth Amendment. They even went so far as to try to blackmail four-star General Charles Whilhem, former chief of the Southern Command, to stop him from testifying for the defense.

There have been attempts to conceal evidence (an 8 mm video, when FBI agent Al Alonso prevented the original from being turned over to the defense; this was a key piece of evidence for the most serious charge in this case).

For us, the prosecutors do not represent the government of the United States, and that is why for us, this is not a case of the Government of the United States vs. Gerardo Hernández. Actually, the prosecution has very skillfully represented the small extremist right-wing sector of the Cuban community, terrorists like José Basulto and organizations like Alpha 66, the Cuban-American National Foundation and Comandos F-4. They even went so far as to embrace and kiss these individuals right in this courtroom, in full view of everyone here. If something about this trial astonished me, it was the tremendous zeal, the unlimited efforts made by the prosecution and all their advisors to faithfully represent this criminal sector, at any cost.

However, the defense has showed truth, dignity and the real stance of the American people towards Cuba. It was the defense that brought in generals and other military and civilians who have contributed to carrying out this policy towards my country, such as: General Charles Whilhem, Admiral Atkinson, Colonel Eugene Carol, Colonel Buckner and Richard Nuccio, former advisor to U.S. President William Clinton on Cuban affairs.

Many of them appeared on a fully voluntary basis, and in this small detail lies a very big message for those willing to understand it.

Ladies and gentlemen: this is a time of major changes; we are well into the 21st century. Today the United States has relations with China. It has relations with Viet Nam, where 56,000 citizens of this country died. It is taking part in talks with North Korea, and many other countries with which it seemed impossible to have relations. Why not with Cuba?

It is true that to carry out our tasks, we needed to resort to unconventional methods. We have done so for obvious reasons of personal security, and never with the intent of harming anyone, or cheating or deceiving anyone, much less the government or institutions of this country.

The evidence is overwhelmingly clear in all respects, then, let us be judged on the basis of that evidence. From the very first day of this trial, we acknowledged our true identities and our responsibilities, but I never accepted, and never will accept, any implication of espionage, or of trying to deceive this country.

I want to express special thanks for the work of our attorneys, for their courage and professionalism. For us, and for everyone, we have won this trial. History will take care of rectifying this verdict, and perhaps this sentence as well.

Gentlemen of the prosecution, whether you like it or not, Cuba is an independent and sovereign country. It has its own legitimate government, its own president, its own martyrs and heroes, and its own convictions. Cuba is not different from the United States. And, gentlemen, Cuba must be respected!

We know that efforts were made to ensure an impartial trial. But the city of Miami is not a place where goals like these can be achieved when it comes to Cuba. Perhaps that was the most critical error in our case: holding the trial in this city.

If preventing the deaths of innocent human beings, defending our two countries from terrorism, and preventing a senseless invasion of Cuba is the reason I am being sentenced today, then, let that sentence be welcomed.

I will wear the prison uniform with the same honor and pride with which a soldier wears his most prized insignia.

This has been a political trial, therefore, we are political prisoners.

All of the evidence is here; this is where history is written. And it is history that will do us true justice.

Thank you.

They defend our dreams — José Omar Torres

Five years after our court statements

It was five years ago, but our denunciation is even more valid today; our denunciation of the unjustified and barbaric actions committed by the US government against our people and against the Five.

In all these years, the US government has not ceased to shamelessly protect the worst terrorists of the Western Hemisphere –Orlando Bosch and Luis Posada Carriles— while continuing to assist the Miami extreme right and trying to break our people with the criminal economic blockade and its threats of military invasion and massive annihilation.

These are all reasons for which we came to the United States to defend our people, and the American people, from death.

Today, like five years ago, we would make exactly the same statements, word for word, more strongly, with many more arguments and greater emphasis challenging the cowardice of the Prosecution and the government, which didn't dare defend their own people from Cuban-American terrorism.

Today, we are stronger, we're better prepared and more convinced of the final victory of truth and justice, and we count on the beautiful and indispensable support of you all, brothers and sisters from all over the world.

And today we continue and shall continue… "to wear the prison uniform with the same honor and pride with which a soldier carries his most prized insignia."

"WE SHALL OVERCOME"

Ramón Labañino Salazar
November 16, 2006
U.S.P. Beaumont, Texas

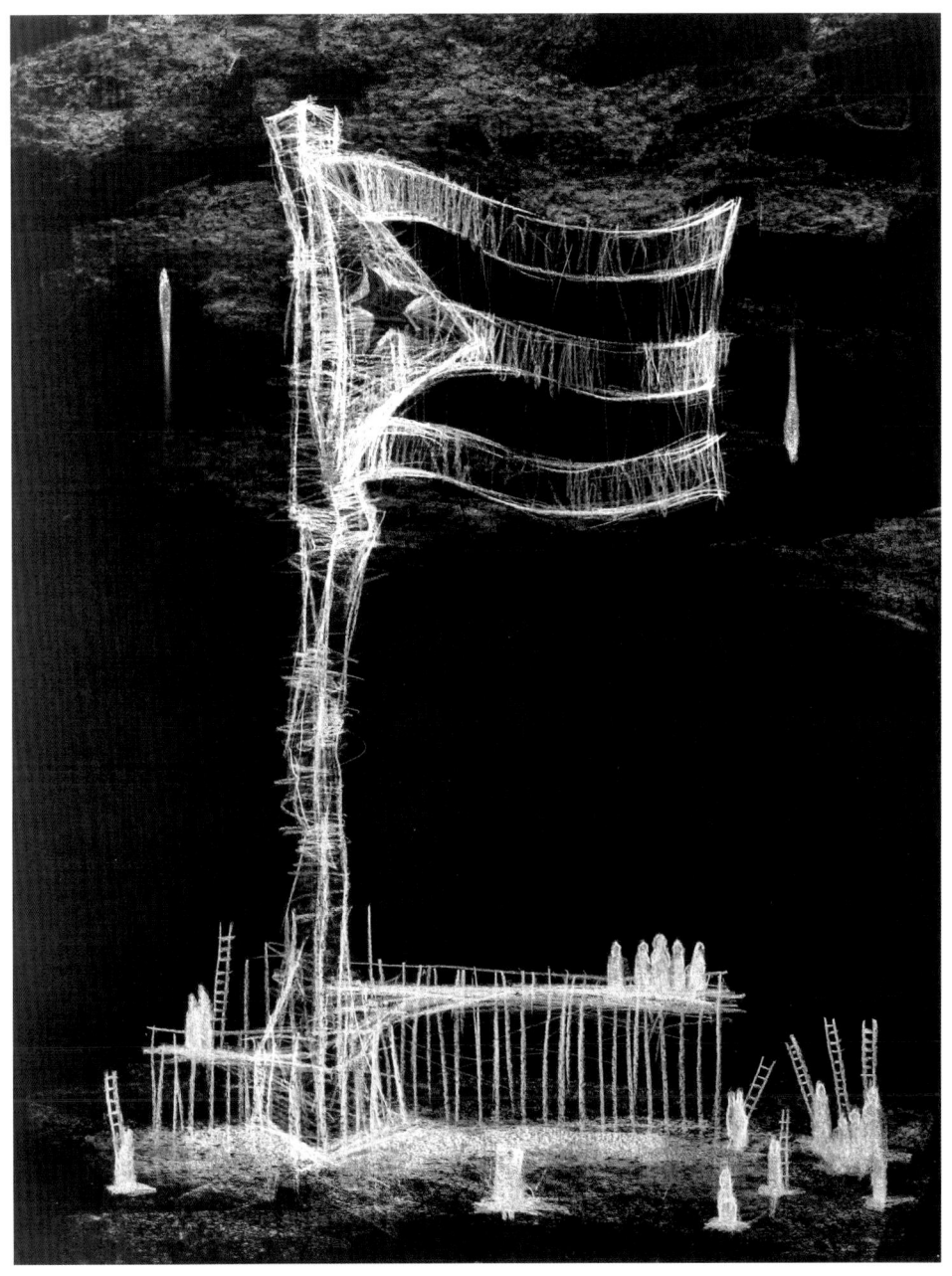

No tittle   Sándor González

pablo armando fernández

stars in the number

To Five imprisoned innocents

Omen of revelations, the number
activates dormant nerves that impel the body.
The hand that labors, feeds, caresses
and the pilgrim foot that surveys and guides,
multiply through activity.
Twin hands and feet fraternize
and in the passing of cycles they
fuse into consummate bonding.
Hearing, touch, taste, flavor and smell
Embody the totality of senses that the soul encompasses.
The lone star with its regal
points, radiates, dictates the destiny
that coincides with those already selected five,
they are hands, feet, senses, beams
that recreate and illuminate the path
from the root to the frond bearing flower and fruit,
in bountiful seed, that restores men's breath
that magnifies free will
the gifts of love.
The prophecies decree:
From the islands voices of freedom will arise singing
to liberate hands, feet and senses
rekindling energy to fasten points on the star.
Five voices in Manhattan,

already free, rescued from Cuba, once imprisoned:
Varela, Heredia, Saco, Villaverde and Martí.
There they seek connections
Older liberated voices,
Franklin, Paine, Jefferson, Hopkinson and Washington.
From this dynamic spectrum in the looming struggle
emerge El H abanero, La Verdad,
El Mensajero semanal, El Independiente,
and *Patria* is born: "To bond and love,
to live in the passion of truth".
Soldiers of deed and word,
guiding and tutoring
in this land that won with force
its own sovereignty
discover those brothers who attach their passion
to the redemptive spirit of warriors.
Those dependable brothers
who turn sacrifice into virtue
and confront conflict
for the love of patria.
When the return became law, the sea
opened its passages to the ship Brothers,
- but the captain reneged, so
emerged the steamer Norstrand -,
to Playitas. And these currents will become the path
of *Granma* from Tuxpan to Las Coloradas.
The body of the patria prepares its defenses,
hands, feet and senses:
Ramón, Gerardo, René, Antonio and Fernando
must remain where danger lurks.
There, the enemy has prepared,
like the captain of the schooner *Brothers*
unfaithful to its own omen.
Symbols of the solitary star
the prisoner heroes resonate with the voices
of Cooper, Hawthorne, Poe, Melville and Whitman
who offered spirit
to the liberated imperial colonies.
Like their predecessors,

from the abyss of darkness forced on each of them,
in solitary, separated,
they detect in these voices of homeland's marrow:
inspiration, support, hands, feet and senses
so that inspired passion protects them from the turbulence
that unleashes fury in deceptive downpours
of dishonest words.
In this alliance they defend the spirit
that in this continent gave birth to a nation
that reveres Whitman and Martí,
Melville and Villaverde, Jefferson and Saco,
Hopkins and Heredia; soil that promised heaven.
Prophecies dictate that the prisoners
shall return: "And give thanks
and resonate with the voice of a rejoicing nation.

Translated by Saul Landau

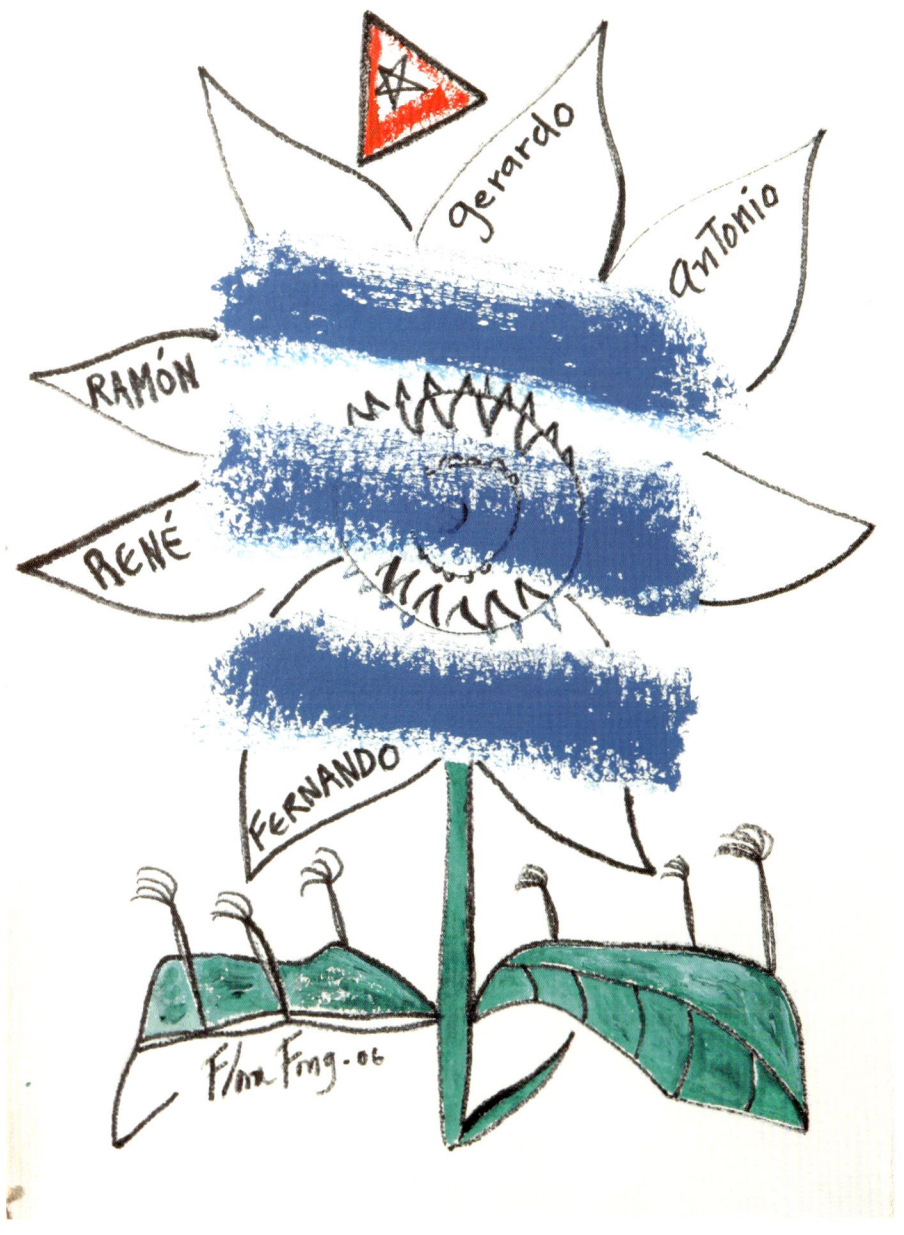

No tittle FLORA FONG

miguel mejides

LEONARDO'S BICYCLE REVISITED

Happiness has a penchant for keeping distance from our place in the world. Today, I feel like playing with the passing of days, my optimism nourished by dreams. I could say plainly and simply that the walls of this prison are no more than a watchtower drawn in my mind or a blue carpet taking me across the deep blue sky. I am one and I am Five, all at the same time; I am ubiquitous. I am an afternoon producing the unassailable harmony of the creatures enclosed for the right to love. And thus, as if with five moves I could change the world where the white horses are not attached to the laws of the unjust men, I am a vernacular Zarathustra or a motionless spirit moving along the path of imagery.

Here, they speak to me in English with signs that I can decipher and turn into birds devouring the beginning of the infinite letters, or in solitude recompose into a system that shapes liberating platonic reasons. That's why when the evening grows murky, when it's not dark but the sun is already asleep, and the earth spins on a glass axis reproducing the infinite, I perceive a palm tree. No one would understand its passionate love; she brings to me the shadows of the people that forged the scope of my memory.

From the distance my lucid mother comes with a child in her arms, and with a quick look I can see that it's me she's carrying, but as ubiquity tends to fade in infallible reproductions my mother holds tight from number Five, the magic number of Hebrews, to repeat that what seems unreal is more than real. Then, for a short while the palm tree becomes an immediate reality, and I find myself inside an inmate's costume, in a hole which is the worst of places where I have spent the most awful days of isolation, after crossing the yard whose stones cooked the stars. And the palm tree fades away for a minute only to come back from the endless distance always promising to speak in a human language.

And so it happens every day when night falls like a harbinger announcing that my pilgrimage is about to start. Then, I become the traveler in a time series arriving at Vinci. I'm taken by a carriage pulled by angels, the landscape an imposed state of the soul, a drama of green olives at twilight. Not far, the dogs are barking and a bronze bell is singing my welcome to an inn. On a book with red pages I write my birthplace, or my birthplaces and my names; the ubiquitous in communion with bodies present everywhere. "You come and go every night," the innkeeper tells me, and I only say, "I come to talk to Leonardo and his artifacts." The innkeeper nods and an indescribable anxiety fills the space. Then I walk to the castle that is now a museum and remorse comes hunting me for I'm running out of time to finish building what I yearn for. Some gringo tourists pass by me discussing the wandering of death in two New York towers. In Spanish I tell them that so has wandered death through my island. But they don't understand; they're too contaminated to get involved.

Once in the castle I walk along, between capitals and astragalus, and the public stays on both sides, sobbing, faced with the eccentricity of something remote that they do not judge. I drag my feet watching window panels that treasure the drawings of machines designed to alleviate the pain, machines that open doors to happiness or to madness. Then I walk down the steps of the old stairs to the moat of the castle; I take a boat and go around the castle navigating in black waters, and coming to a confluence I suddenly go against an oak door inlaid with granite. I knock the agreed signal and say the slogan of the libertarian circle nobody can destroy, then I hear the bolt take its lucky turns and an old man tells me the latest wood is ready for the work.

I humbly go to a corner looking at the numberless pieces I have been building in weeks; if I persevere I'll finish this day the work that will take us to freedom and that no law will abduct. An oil painting of a woman with eyes that resemble the old man's is gazing at me from the far corner of the hall, her enigmatic smile apparently saying she can understand everything in a heroic concept of divinity. That smile also predicts that the sin of the worst mortal shall contaminate every creature. The woman looks at me; she guides my exultation and pushes my hand that will shape the wood like a carpenter using his plane to laboriously shape the handlebars of a bicycle.

The moonlight breaks through the window and I see Vinci like a silver port whose compass will take us to a road leading neither north nor south. How many people live in Vinci? I wonder while I watch the old man who never looks at the woman in the oil painting, the same old man that is now –if there is a now— drawing a God of infinite faces as if possessed by the passion of a heretical anxious to expose the dagger that inspires humans to become killers. "Fifteen-hundred souls live here now," the old man says in answer to my thoughts, "but when I was born we were barely two-hundred mortals. My mother made pasta with hard semolina and sang, in a dialect, a song of vindication and eternity that alluded to the history of five men turned into one and one building a bird of immortal wood." "Leonardo's bird," I say. "No," he responds, "the bird we all carry inside as a universe of liberating dreams, the mellow sound of a guitar that changes the everlasting condition of the moments, a bird of wood that likes being caressed to become the intimate resurrection of the wishes to wake up in the arms of the woman we love and the children who will perceive what you're now building as the essence of clover brought back by their parents." "Today is the day," I hopefully say. "It's up to you," he responds, "cause five sacred words shall be silently pronounced, as if you were reading *The Iliad* inside yourself, and then, maybe, the miracle will happen…" "And what about the woman in the oil painting?" I ask. "You see," the old man complains, "you're fond of small chat. But let me say this, the woman is just that, a woman, or perhaps she was a poor being who fed the lions of the Roman circus with her own flesh or a prostitute whose smile could annul the poisonous lust. It's not me, let that be clear. I always sleep with my face exposed to the moon to make me invulnerable to whatever is more than human in physical beauty; I'm just a snake charmer who's acquainted with the horror of men in your century. So, finish your work and go with the wind of your legend!"

    I was tired but I went on carving the wood, giving it the shape that would finally have the entire rigor and the stubbornness of my last night of work. Thus the hours die one by one under the midnight rain falling on Vinci, a rain like a midday downpour on an island. Step by step the bicycle was growing a heart that turned it into an immortal instrument. It struck me that my tenderness with her was acquiring an indoctrinating presence. The bicycle looked like one of those stolid treaties the ancients used to account to their deities. My hands as guided by chance gave shape to balance; the recently finished handlebars resembled the horns of a deer; the wheels of cypress's stumps were like the fortune demanded by the invisible drawing of roads; the chained one like a memory of metal forms wrecked in the Aegean sea; and the best, an oil lamp that would light the destiny coming at dawn. The work was now finished; the ghosts had delivered, the elegiac, as Leonardo would say in awe and admiration watching his dream turned into wood muscles.

    We were The Five striving to come out into the omniscience to fete. The sorcerer in the oil painting was also excited and her smile said something in a language that reminded me of the Aramaic or was it perhaps only a good-fortune prayer for the escapees. The old man started talking again to say that because we had fought against gun powder, we had suffered and that now, the gun powder in the wind would take us back home. The end is coming, which is the beginning, he said, and there are no images, only memories. Then, as if driven by the madness of the mad dogs fighting rabies, Leonardo cut the canvass for the candles and added them to our bicycle. It was now a light boat crossing the seas of China, a new sail boat with a figurehead whose image reproduced the astrology of Universe. "You dreamed it like that, and you, in your fantasies, made it real," the old man from Vinci said, Leonardo the genius, the sinner, the enlightened. The merit will go to the olive-green rooster when it flies singing a song that only the chosen ones will hear. At that moment he also said that in the secular prison cells of America there will only be bodies, subtle symbols like copies of the figures that you were, every one of you.

The jail-keepers will lack the necessary sanity to understand that Five creatures embody the righteousness which brings rejoicing. Thence, Leonardo infected us with his spirit and the sails were blown by the morning wind; meanwhile, we pedaled on our bicycle up to the sky, and the rooster launched an inaudible whistle. The olive groves became an immortal landscape, the castle hoisted a flag with a palm tree on it and the sea expanded like a blue door. Then, the imperfect silence filled us with excitement. The bicycle was flying over Havana on a January 14th in one of the years close to 2000.

cintio vitier

ramón

Like Martí's political prison
is yours, Ramón, and of those of our race.
Perhaps you did not know. Today his hand
moves forward with yours. He embraces you.

In this case a new trial was called for given the perfect storm created when the wave of intensive emotions in the Miami community and the wide publicity, both before and during the trial, combined with the Prosecution's inappropriate remarks.

IN THE LIGHT OF ALL THE ARGUMENTS, THE DEFENDANTS' SENTENCES ARE REPEALED AND WE ORDER THE REALIZATION OF A NEW TRIAL.

11th Circuit Court of Appeals
Atlanta, August 9, 2005

The three magistrates on the panel bring to the case a professional experience in the excess of 80 years. Their decision was argued in a 93-pages document.

On September 29, 2005, in a completely unusual move, according to American legal experts, the United States government filed an appeal urging the Atlanta Court's three judges' ruling to be reconsidered by a full 12 judge's panel.

On August 9, 2006, exactly one year to the day that a three judge's panel in the Atlanta Court unanimously decided to repeal the sentences of the Cuban Five, a full member panel from the same Court, by a majority vote, recanted from that decision, thus ratifying the sentences and denying the realization of a new trial.

THE LEGAL PROCESS AGAINST THE FIVE CONTINUES TO BE DELAYED. ON SEPTEMBER 12, IT WILL BE NINE YEARS SINCE THE ARREST OF FIVE MEN WHO SHOULD HAVE NEVER BEEN IMPRISONED AND WHO DESPITE THEIR INNOCENCE ARE STILL INCARCERATED IN THE UNITED STATES AND CONFINED TO MAXIMUM SECURITY PRISONS. THEIR CONTACTS WITH THEIR FAMILIES ARE LIMITED BY THE CONTINUOUS DELAYS IN ISSUING VISAS. THIS IS WORSE IN THE CASES OF OLGA SALANUEVA AND ADRIANA PÉREZ WHO HAVE NOT SEEN THEIR HUSBANDS FOR TEN YEARS SINCE THEY HAVE BEEN REPEATEDLY DENIED THE VISAS.

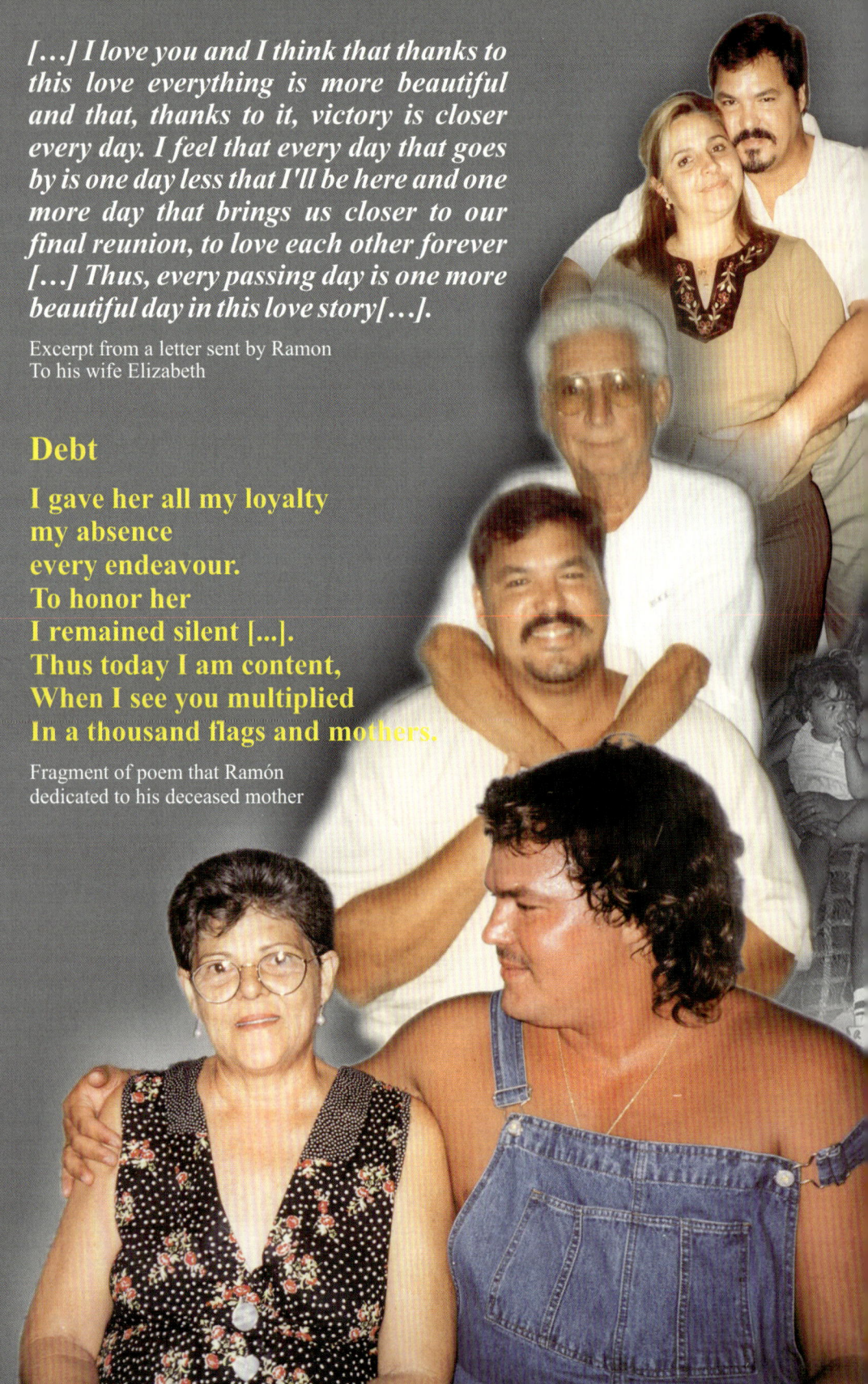

[…] I love you and I think that thanks to this love everything is more beautiful and that, thanks to it, victory is closer every day. I feel that every day that goes by is one day less that I'll be here and one more day that brings us closer to our final reunion, to love each other forever […] Thus, every passing day is one more beautiful day in this love story[…].

Excerpt from a letter sent by Ramon
To his wife Elizabeth

Debt

I gave her all my loyalty
my absence
every endeavour.
To honor her
I remained silent [...].
Thus today I am content,
When I see you multiplied
In a thousand flags and mothers.

Fragment of poem that Ramón
dedicated to his deceased mother

Letter to my daughters

My dearest daughters:
Now you understand why Dad couldn't spend more time with you, or live so many happy and joyful moments as other dads do with their children […] I'm sorry for not being there, because I couldn't be with Mom during her pregnancies, and I was not there when you were born, because I was not there when you first opened your eyes, and I couldn't change your diapers or help you take your first steps […] and because the youngest of you hardly knows me […]. But you should know that I had to go for this love I feel for you and for all, and that wherever I've been or will be, you've always been and forever will be with me […] I'll be back, don't you doubt it […] and when I return we shall build together every dream and desire that we had to put on hold […]

    See you soon,
    Daddy Ramón

To my daughters

*I granted them their lives,
splashed their love with dew,
magnified their souls in mine
and their issues made me grow.*

*My lone life has become three,
so three are my wishes and
my fates,
three my grateful merriment,
three my fortunes and my plans.
I would live only for you
my whole self and what I am.
I am so far from you today
thus I cannot enjoy your
happiness,
but you should know how much
I love you
wherever I am,
wherever I am,
I shall live eternally for you!*

December 21st, 2001.
E. D. C. Miami FL.
11th Floor, West Wing, Cell 6 (upper part)

To you who are waiting

To you Ely, because love conquers all

*To you who are waiting
On the warm wetness
Of my last kiss,
Over the waves of a tender
Flow of passions.*

*To you who are waiting
for the right moment
to embrace nostalgia
and ease every second
of this eternal waiting.*

*To you who are waiting
come hell or high water
have faith and keep fighting
beat everything and everyone,
remember it is two of us battling
in this long waiting,
and after we reach our victory
we will get back
all our debts.*

November 1st, 2003
U. S. P. Beaumont, Texas

Dearest Laurita:

I want that the moment you receive this letter, when you touch it you feel that I am in every letter, every colon, every period and every sigh. I'm giving you a very big kiss to tell you I love you, very, very much, endlessly my beautiful girl, my baby girl, my precious, mine, mine […] but I promise that I will put behind us all this time that I have not been there, I without your love and you without mine, without being able to educate you, to teach you how to read and write, and so many things about life that I want you to know […]

Your Daddy. I love you.

Sometimes

"The meaning of ow lives (5) is the love to our people".

Yes, it is true
Sometimes
It feels hard to wake up
having nothing of what you love
but among all you hate.

Sometimes
it feels hard to be without you
without your lips
without your warm hugs
or without your silhouette
stuck to mine
in each free space.

Sometimes
it is painful to long for
my daughters by my side
to look forward hopelessly
to an "I love you" or a "Dad",
to dream of a sweet kiss
or an innocent tear I could
wipe away gently
and lovingly.

Sometimes
it feels hard to desire
to be surrounded by people
by the laugh of children
by the joy on the streets
by the warm breeze of our coasts
by the unbelievable green
of our mountains.

Sometimes
it feels hard to yearn to be
walking barefoot
along the white sand
or swimming onthe intense blue
of our ocean
so it wipes away our griefs.

Sometimes
it feels hard to wish
to see our flag fluttering
flowered with martyrs and heroes
in some square
of our island.

Sometimes
It feels so hard
to wake up here
longing to be there
and this I cannot deny…

But I also understand
quite well
how hard and heroic it is:
to fight against an unmeasured
gigantic injustice
against a rich and mean power
against a modern Neo-Fascism
to protect our peoples
against the crimes of an Empire.

This is why
sometimes
even when it is hard to wake up
here
I deeply appreciate
living and fighting this Mission
which allows us to recognize
much better the meaning of:

the adverb   Faithfully
the verb   I fight
the noun   Homeland
and the optimism in the slogan
"Venceremos!"

February 24th, 2006

[1] Cuban slogan to finish political speeches: "We will win"

> Other people's terrorist actions cannot excuse the wrong and illegal conduct of this or any other defendant.

Judge Joan Lenard. Taken from the sentence hearing, December 14, 2001

We will continue to appeal to those values, and to the American people's vocation for truth. And we will do so with all the patience, faith and courage that we draw from the crime of dignity.

RENÉ

nancy morejón

TWO BIRDS, ONE SONG

This is a love story, but the real story behind this love only started when these lovers were confronted with unspeakable obstacles and misfortunes, including the arbitrary legal actions that have kept them helplessly apart for over eight years. The protagonists of this story are Olga Salanueva Arango and René González Sehwerert, a young couple who had rather easily founded a family.

René was born into a family of Cuban immigrants in Chicago, the famous windy city, on August 13, 1956. He enjoyed the simple pleasures of childhood near the lakes that saw the beginning of his life. Later, in 1961, his parents decided to relocate in Havana. René was still a teenager when he became a rather appreciated pilot instructor. On April 17, 1983 he married Olga, an industrial engineer he met through a common acquaintance at one of the blue beaches east of the capital. It was love at first sight, its power probably stemming from the intensive light on that tropical coastline.

From then on a very special bond brought together Olga and René, two valued professionals in their respective areas. They were never apart; both at home and on the streets, they were like those birds that oblivious of their surroundings build a love nest or fly through stormy clouds and thunderstorms towards dawn, their beaks and legs, heads and wings hard to tell apart. It was a couple fashioned in the image of those birds that perch on any tree for a mesmerizing dance that even heavens cannot help envying.

One year into their marriage their first daughter, Irmita, was born. Then, on a regular afternoon of 1996, when the daily routine with its unavoidable burden began to settle in their lives, the wandering instincts of a deeply-rooted centuries-old tradition, dating back to their Hebrew origins, led them out of Cuba to resettle at the city of Miami, in South Florida. The first winds of an ancient pilgrim ritual had blown them away.

But the true story of Olga and René would start with a sinister episode, on September 12, 1998, when their second daughter Ivette, —born at the Jackson Memorial Hospital, the only public hospital in Miami— was barely more than four months old. René had just come home after a long working day, and in need of rewarding his spirit and taking some rest, he approached the baby to hold her and feed her a bottle of milk. In a short while the baby was asleep, comfortably sprawled on her father's chest.

Minutes later, curious about the perfect silence and wishing to join in, Olga walked into the room where she found a wonderful oasis. Her first thought was how to capture that loving show of happiness; she then looked around and spotted a small camera left on a nearby dresser the week before. At that moment, Olga and René could not guess the full significance of that picture taken on the night of September 12; a night not different from any other. They were blissfully unaware that sometime later that tender, unrehearsed picture would bring nourishment to the soul, the spirit and the flesh of René González Sehwerert.

At dawn the following day, FBI agents would unexpectedly break into that home, drastically and violently entering that room full of love and caring, with the intent to put a happy father under arrest. This contented father was totally unsuspecting of his immediate fate. René could not know that his physical and moral integrity would not only be threatened, beleaguered and trampled on by systematic abuse but also by derision and the strictest confinement. By the end of February 2002, René was transferred from the Miami Federal Detention Center to various American penitentiaries.

At the time Olga was granted resident status she received a social security number and was asked, "*How do you want your name registered?*" "*Just as it is,*" she said, not knowing the consequences this would have for her immediate future. When René was arrested and Olga started to file her claims, the reply was that they did not share the same family name so they could not know if she was his lawful wife. It was a treacherous argument. She had to file a request for her marriage certificate in Havana since the one kept at their downtown apartment assaulted by the Federal agents had been lost never to be found again.

"*One August 13, on René's birthday, I visited him in jail. I found him rather uneasy, as if many thoughts were crammed into his head and he didn't know where to begin. Yet, his first question was about the letter from the District Attorney's office. I quickly asked him, 'What's that letter from the District Attorney's office?' René started to explain that it was a letter in which the District Attorney's office tried to bribe him. They offered not to indict him if he agreed to declare himself guilty and to take part in the trial as a witness for the Prosecution.*

"In the last paragraph of that letter special emphasis was made on the migratory status of our family, particularly on my permanent resident status in the United States, so it was very likely that I would be indicted, too. Of course, René didn't accept the deal offered by the Prosecution. What followed? Well, they came for me; I was arrested three days after my visit to the Federal Detention Center.

"I was so tense that night that I could hardly sleep. Then at daybreak, about 6:00 am, I looked at the alarm clock. I could see cracks of light filtering through the window shutters. I could hardly get off the bed. They knocked on the door, hard, very hard. As I was walking down the hall to the apartment's main door, the Feds were knocking it down to take me into custody. They were two Immigration and Naturalization Services' agents. I was alone, very much alone."

There were no greetings or introductions, only a sharp question, "Where are your daughters?" But they were not interested in the girls' whereabouts, they did not care; they only wanted to verify her true relationship with René. Based on the theory that Olga's family name did not match René's, they challenged her resident status, which they first kept secret from her and later totally ignored. Irmita was on vacation with her grandparents in Cuba. Ivette was in Sarasota, cared for by Teté, her great-grandmother on the father's side. René had been in prison for two years.

Olga Salanueva was taken from her rented apartment in Miami to the Lauderdale state prison. "Do you need to make a call?" said in perfect Spanish an agent less rude than the others. She immediately called René's grand uncle for him to let the great-grandmother know about her present situation. The over eighty-year-old great-grandmother, who took care of Ivette during the week for Olga to be able to work, must have been very anxious since the first thing Olga did every morning was to call her for news of the baby. As in those first moments Olga's phone calls were unrestricted and she was making a local call, she spoke at length with Teté.

"Do you want to see René?" the same agent said, again in perfect Spanish. Olga nodded and still thinking it would not happen, as in an afterthought, she uttered the word 'yes'. Something deep inside told her that this would be one of her few chances to meet with *Rene*, thinking of his name with the stress on the first syllable, as she intimately called him. Only two hours had passed since the proposal was first made and Olga was already at the Miami Federal Detention Center dressed in the dirtiest and more deteriorated uniform her jail keepers could find.

They brought René. When they were face to face, they furtively exchanged glances, each knowing what to do. They would not be enticed or manipulated; they would not let their stream of sweet memories to dry up; they would not let their captors cross the threshold into their inner worlds, their deep love and vivid affection for each other. They would not let their captors carry any of that away like hurricane winds blow the birds off trees.

Olga, René and their daughters would not let these paid bullies disturb their minds or their spirits. The latter intended to fulfill their threatening promise: saving one family to destroy five. Neither Olga nor René felt they were victims of an ordinary scheme or an outrageous, unprecedented action in the constitutional history of the United States. They responded to their enemies like the faithful birds they are. They were undaunted. Nothing would make them show their deep sorrow, even if at that place and moment they could feel the tearing separation seemingly attained by their captors. They were still the same birds from that tropical blue beach east of Havana.

Standing there, face to face, there was only this precise phrase that Olga heard from René: *"The orange color sits well with you,"* and his eyes were warning her of all the possible risks: the most imminent being deportation to Cuba. A sweet smile showed on Olga's face but her guards' expression was one of deep bitterness. Olga and René kissed and said good-bye; they could not know that a long time would pass before they met again.

"I don't know when I'll see René again." This was the thought cutting through her skin at dawn. Not seeing René again was then a premonition but it would become a sad reality, because the proceedings that started on August 16 in the year 2000 would be marred by a murky atmosphere, with no direction or end in sight.

In her severe prison, Olga learned to do without the rush of urban life and the company of her husband and daughters. She learned that physical solitude can be tempered by the resistance that brings relief with the incense of the truth defended. The paths she walked to ease her pain led her to understand that words can save human beings forcibly held incommunicado. She wrote letters to René, many letters. *"Writing these letters is like opening a window on our lives,"* Olga wrote, unsuspecting that her letters would be windows without a view, shut down by her prison guards. Although she wrote in her tiniest handwriting on any paper she could lay her hands on, all the energy she poured into it could not prevent the brutality of her enemies. Those letters written while she was in prison would never reach René, they were all intercepted.

A woman had been imprisoned, snatched from her home, censored; a mother had been banished to the loneliest attic. Her letters were "lost" to some kind of black magic concocted in the darkest cellar. A mother, a father and two fragile daughters entangled in a cobweb of traps that have failed —and will fail— to make them loose direction.

From September 12, 1998, the lives of Olga and René have moved along parallel lines as if these unmatched lovers had chosen a path of love that takes them apart and while the world around them continues its journey into a new century, every road leads them to another prison, to inconceivable isolation. Yet, their love has grown stronger, more tangible.

What century is this? What is this century we are living where a woman cannot meet her man because his captors arrest and detain her to frighten him, to try to bribe him into betraying his comrades? After her release from jail and deportation to Cuba, her country of birth, Olga Salanueva Arango entered proudly the endless labyrinth of filing visa applications that would allow her and her daughters to visit René in whatever prison he might be, whether McKean and Loreto in Pennsylvania; Edgefield in South Carolina; or Marianna in Florida, the latter being a mid-security penitentiary sixty eight miles off Tallahassee. But, every visa application filed by Olga Salanueva has been systematically turned down.

One of the scariest experiences is that for seventeen months René never had the benefit of a due process. Meanwhile, he waited in a sort of diabolic limbo known as *solitary confinement*; one of the most sophisticated forms of mental and physical torture, which sharpens the sensitivity of the victim, as the daily mortification turns his body into his own house. This kind of imprisonment, which violates the basic right to *habeas corpus,* focuses its devastating action on the victim's senses for it makes him feel that nothing else exists but his body, that he cannot walk, that he can hardly move or look around. It's hard to even try to imagine that limited space where only the body of the inmate fits. It's like the toilets in some train stations or home restaurants where one can hardly sit or stand. This type of *solitary confinement* the inmates call it *the hole*. Here, the victims' self-respect is assaulted and devalued on a daily basis.

Olga Salanueva recounts that in the seventeen months that René was kept in solitary confinement he could only see their younger daughter twice. *"He saw her once in May, when Ivette was thirteen months old. He was sitting handcuffed to the chair. He could not even touch the baby. The second time he was not handcuffed; apparently they realized they had gone too far the first time. In those seventeen months he could only see her again through a tiny glass window in the hole. At the time he assumed I could be passing by, he would lean out and look down; his cell was on the twelfth floor and Ivette was no more than a little speck in her mother's arms"*.[1]

---

[1] Olga Salanueva's testimony for Letters of Love and Hope: The Story of the Cuban Five, introduced by Alice Walter. Preface by Nancy Morejón. Havana, ed. José Martí, 2004, p. 28.

From the year 2000, when Olga Salanueva Arango was deported to Cuba, she has been systematically denied an entry visa to the United States. Seven times, consecutively, the US government has refused to issue her a visa. Thus, Olga has been prevented from visiting René and he from receiving Olga and their youngest daughter Ivette who he had not seen again since September 12, 1998, when she was no more than a baby.

After seven years of waiting, and due to the prolonged delay of their legal process, every time René spoke with Olga on the phone he insisted on the possibility of Ivette visiting him in prison. The girl, who is eight years old now, wanted to see her father, too. Under the circumstances, the whole family undertook to making all possible efforts for Ivette to be able to visit her father accompanied by her sister Irmita who is over eighteen now. The whole family agreed to take measures that would ensure the little girl adequate professional care to prepare her spirits and her traumatized mind for such an encounter. It is a shocking experience, even for an adult, to visit a prison center given the adverse surroundings in a place where people are incarcerated.

The encounter, which happened on Saturday, December 30, 2006 at the Marianna prison center in Florida, was very moving both for the father and the little girl, despite the hostile conditions in which such visits take place. Father and daughter managed to ignore the hostile circumstances and immediately communicated with the spontaneous affection that usually exists between parents and their children. It was a very meaningful and rewarding experience for both but Olga Salanueva, the exemplary mother, could not be there although in all these years that René has remained unjustly incarcerated, she has been the basic pillar in a home that is hurt but still alive and genuine.

The last time that Olga saw René was on the eve of his trial, on August 16 of the year 2000, the same day she was arrested. Olga does not know when she will be able to see him again and to visit him with their two daughters.

Almost ten years have passed, but beyond the iron bars of his prison cell Olga and René continue to be bonded by an umbilical cord that no political system can cut. And, together with their daughters, the grandmothers and grandfathers, they will forever be an exceptional family. Olga and René are two birds that God wanted to place in this world and, rather sooner than later, they will live together in their nest.

Havana, January 6, 2007

No tittle   ENRIQUE ÁVILA

Defense statement presented by René González Sehwerert at the sentencing hearing held friday, december 14, 2001

Before I begin, I would like to propose an experiment to those present in the courtroom today: close your eyes, and imagine that you are in downtown New York. Now, when the first firefighter comes along, look him straight in the eye, very seriously, and tell him to his face that nothing happened on September 11. That it is all a lie. Nothing but camera tricks. It is all pure paranoia and propaganda. At this point, if neither your own shame, nor the poor firefighter, has made you swallow your words, then you are eminently qualified to have been a prosecutor in this case.

And now, with the permission of this Court, I will begin.

Your Honor:

Months ago, in one of her efforts to sweep the subject of terrorism against Cuba under the carpet, using the twisted logic of her confused argument on intent and motivation, Mrs. Heck Miller told the court that we could leave the political speeches until this point in the trial. Even back then, when all of the prosecutors' political hatred had been unleashed on us through the conditions of our confinement, the manipulation of the evidence, and, even worse, the use and abuse of my own family to blackmail, hurt and humiliate me, I was far from imagining just how important it would be for the prosecution in this case to pour out all of their political rancor towards us.

Nevertheless, after six months of listening to these same prosecutors shoving their prejudices down the jury's throats over and over again, I can still tell Mrs. Heck Miller that she was wrong. I do not need to speak of my political beliefs, which I do not in any way renounce, to say that I condemn terrorism, that I condemn war, and that I feel profound contempt for those people, so completely obsessed with their hatreds and petty interests, who have devoted so much time to harming their country by promoting terrorism and fostering a war on which they squander all the courage that they do not have and that others will need, also their victims, on the battlefield.

I do not need to talk politics, to say that I believe that innocent people should not have to die for this, neither in Cuba, nor here in the United States, nor anywhere else in the world. And I would do what I did and take the risks that I took for any country in the world, including the United States, regardless of political considerations.

I firmly believe that you can be a Catholic and be a good person, that you can be a Jew and be a good person, that you can be a capitalist, a Muslim or a communist and be a good person; but there is no such thing as a good person who is also a terrorist. You must be sick to be a terrorist, just as you must be sick to believe that there is such a thing as a good terrorist.

Unfortunately, not everyone feels the same way. When it comes to Cuba, the rules apparently change, and some people think that terrorism and war are good things to do. And so we have a prosecutor like Mr. Kastrenakes who defends José Basulto's right to break the law as long as it is announced on television. We have an expert on terrorism like Mr. Hoyt, who believes that ten explosions in a one-year period would constitute a wave of terrorism in Miami, but not in Havana. We have an air safety expert for whom the acts of provocation perpetrated by Brothers to the Rescue against Havana, widely publicized on television, would be a different thing if they were perpetrated against Washington, because they would be, according to him, more urgent and verifiable. We have people who for 40 years have publicly advertised themselves as terrorists, yet the prosecutors to my left only seem to have noticed it when they testified in this case for the defense. Agents Angel Berlinguerí and Héctor Pesquera, the latter no less than the head of the local FBI, proudly appear as guests on the same radio stations, with the same people and on the same programs that violate federal laws by openly raising funds to organize terrorist activities or defend terrorists around the world.

Meanwhile, Mrs. Caroline Heck Miller calls for these nice terrorists to be judged in heaven, while Mr. Frómeta, after trying to buy nothing more than a couple of surface-to-air missiles, antitank weapons and a bit of highly potent explosive, is considered a good father, a good citizen and a good person, who might deserve something like a year of house arrest from the South Florida District Attorney's Office. This, your Honor, as far as I know, is called hypocrisy, and it is also criminal.

And when this same office fights to keep me in a Special Housing Unit for as long as possible, when my family is used as an instrument to break my will, when my daughters are only allowed to see their father twice during the 17 months of this isolation and the only way I can watch the first steps taken by my little girl is through a 12th floor window, then I can only feel proud of being here, and I can only thank the prosecutors for giving me this opportunity to confirm that I am on the right track, that the world still needs a lot of improving, and that the best thing for the people of Cuba is to keep the island clean of the element that has taken over so many souls here in Miami. I want to thank them for allowing me to prove myself against their hatred and resentment, and for this pride I feel after having lived through the most intense, useful, important and glorious days of my life, when this courtroom seemed too small to hold all of the truths spoken, and we watched them squirming with impotence as they fought to hide each and every one of those truths.

And if an apology will make them happy, then I will offer them one: I am very sorry that I was unable to tell their agents that I was cooperating with the Cuban government. If they had an honest stance towards terrorism, I could have done so, and together we could have found a solution to the problem. When I think of those endless discussions about the specific intent to break the law, I realize that this situation goes far beyond the question of whether failing to register oneself is illegal or not. And that is because, unfortunately, even if foreign agents could advertise in the yellow pages here without being registered beforehand, we, being Cubans, would have to remain incognito for such basic tasks as neutralizing terrorists or drug traffickers, something we should be doing together, if a logical approach could prevail. I am also sorry if the anti-Castro affiliation of the criminals I fought brought them closer to certain officials or members of the Attorney General's Office. I feel very badly about this, honestly.

Actually, this whole issue of Cuban agents has a very simple solution: Leave Cuba alone. Do your job. Respect the sovereignty of the Cuban people. I would gladly send every last spy back to the island. We have better things to do there, all of them a lot more constructive than watching the criminals who freely walk the streets of Miami.

I do not want to pass up this opportunity to address myself to the many good people we have had the chance to meet during this trial.

First of all, I want to thank the U.S. Marshals for their professional behavior, their decency, their courtesy and their anonymous sacrifice. There were times when we good-naturedly sympathized with each other for being the only people in the courtroom whose needs were not taken into account in the time schedules, and we all laughed together about it. But they were always disciplined and did their duties well.

I also want to thank the translators, Larry, Richard and Lisa. They did a first-class job and were always available whenever our families or we needed their services. I offer them my sincerest gratitude for their hard work and decency towards everyone. It must be a privilege for this court to have a team like them. My best wishes to Mr. Londergan as well.

I also wish to extend my deepest respect to the members of the U.S. military who testified, whether for the prosecution or the defense, and who spoke sincerely, as well as to the officials, experts and agents who were honest. I would have liked to see more honesty among the latter group, and I would have gladly acknowledged it here.

To all of them, who could very well represent the best of the American people, I extend my highest regards and my assurances that there is an entire nation of people just a step to the south from here who do not harbor the slightest animosity towards their big northern neighbor. Individuals who either do not know, or do not want to know, or are not interested in knowing what Cuba really is have, systematically slandered those people, and that country, throughout this trial. I am going to take the liberty of reading an excerpt from a letter written by my wife on July 30:

"René, there are constant shows of support here for us, the families, and for all of you. Yesterday, when I took bus 58 home from Mom's house, a number of people recognized me, and Yvette was talking to everyone. Because it's carnival time, the bus filled right up when we went through Centro Habana, and Yvette decided to act up when it was time for us to get off; she sat herself down on the stairs of the bus and refused to get up. You can imagine what it was like, the bus full of people, me bouncing around trying to pick her up and not being able to, Yvette glued to her spot and everyone pushing. Then a woman came up to me; she squeezed my hand and gave me a prayer card she had suddenly pulled out of her purse, entitled, "A Happy Home". And she said, 'At my church we pray for the five every day, and we pray for their children to have a happy home, like Jesus did, because they were over there so that all children would have a happy home as well.'

"She kind of caught me by surprise, I almost didn't have time to thank her because I had to get off the bus quickly, but I realized that this is the way we Cubans are. And today we are more united than ever, regardless of beliefs or religions, everyone with their own faith, but all united in the same cause. I am going to keep the prayer card as a memento."

I feel obliged to stop reading here to clarify that I am not a religious person. I do not want the prosecution to distort my words later and claim that I have brought God into this courtroom out of hypocrisy.

Your Honor:

As you can see, even to talk about Cuba I do not need to air my political beliefs here. Others have done it in the framework of this trial throughout three years, oozing irrational hatred. And this hatred is even more absurd when you realize that it has been bred at a gut level, that it is a visceral hatred aimed at something that they simply do not know. It is truly sad to be taught to hate something that you do not even know.

And so there have been people here speaking with impunity against Cuba, offending a nation of people whose only crime is having chosen their own path, and having defended that choice successfully, at the cost of enormous sacrifices. I am not going to give anyone the benefit of distracting myself with all the lies told here about Cuba, but I will refer to one that was so monstrous as to amount to disrespect for this courtroom and the jury:

When Mr. Kastrenakes stood up and said, in front of this symbol of American justice, that we had come here to destroy the United States, he showed how little that symbol and that justice matter to him, and he also showed how little respect he had for the jury. Unfortunately, he was right with regard to the latter.

Neither the evidence in this case, or history, or our beliefs, nor the education we received supports the absurd idea that Cuba wants to destroy the United States. The problems of the human race cannot be resolved by destroying any country; for too many centuries, empires have been destroyed only for similar or worse empires to be built on their ruins. Any threat to this nation is not going to come from a people like the people of Cuba, where it is considered immoral to burn a flag, whether it is from the United States or any other country.

If you allow me, as a descendant of industrious and hard-working Americans, with the privilege of having been born in this country and the privilege of having grown up in Cuba, I would tell the noble American people not to look so far to the south to find the threat to the United States.

Cling to the real and genuine values that inspired the founding fathers of this nation. The lack of these values, pushed aside by other less idealistic interests, is the real threat to this society. Power and technology can become a weakness if they are not in the hands of cultured people, and the hatred and ignorance we have seen here towards a small country, which nobody here knows, can be dangerous when combined with a blinding sense of power and false superiority. Go back to Mark Twain and forget about Rambo if you really want to leave your children a better country. Every alleged Christian who was brought up here to lie after swearing on the Bible is a threat to this country, in view of the way their conduct served to undermine these values.

Your Honor:

Having written these words in preparation for my sentencing, scheduled for September 26, the tragic and horrendous crimes of September 11 have obliged me to add a few reflections that I cannot fail to share with this Court. I must be very tactful, to ensure that nobody can accuse me of capitalizing on these abominable acts in my own favor. But there are times when we must speak certain truths, no matter how painful they may be. It is very much like telling a son or daughter, a brother or sister, when they have made a mistake, and we want, out of love, to help them avoid making that same mistake in the future. It is in that spirit that I want to speak through you with this message to the American people.

The seeds of the tragedy that has plunged this nation into mourning today were sown many years ago. We were led to believe that by shooting down civilian planes and bombing schools, in a place as distant as it was unknown, certain individuals were fighting for freedom, simply because they were fighting communism. I would never blame the American people for that lack of vision; but those who provided the missiles and created an image of those people that did not match their criminal acts were also committing the crime of hypocrisy.

And I am not looking back into the past to rub it in anyone's face. I merely want to invite you to look at the present and reflect on the future, by sharing the following reflection with this court: "Yesterday's hypocrisy is to today's tragedy what today's hypocrisy will be to tomorrow's tragedy." We all have a responsibility towards our children, which goes beyond political prejudices or the petty need to earn a salary, hold on to an ephemeral political post or ingratiate ourselves with a handful of tycoons. That responsibility obliges us to put aside today's hypocrisy, so that we can give them a tomorrow free of tragedies.

They have sought to judge the five of us in the name of this hypocrisy, and now that it is my turn to face my sentence, I realize that, unlike my comrades, I do not even have the right to consider myself a victim. They way in which I conducted myself perfectly coincides with the description offered in the charges brought against me. If I have come to this trial, it is out of solidarity with my brothers, and in order to speak certain truths and refute the lies with which the prosecution tried to exaggerate my activities and present me as a danger to American society.

Therefore, I do not even have the right to ask for clemency at a moment like this, a moment at which this court will have seen who knows how many converts, some genuine, others false, some finding God after signing a pact with the Devil, all of them using this podium to show their repentance. I cannot judge them, and each will know what to do with his dignity. I also know what to do with mine, and I would like to believe that you would understand that I have no reason to repent.

Yet, I will always feel obliged to ask for justice for my comrades, accused of crimes they did not commit and sentenced on the basis of prejudices by a jury that passed up a unique opportunity to make a difference. They never attempted to obtain any secrets from this country, and as for the most monstrous accusation, it was merely a matter of a patriot defending the sovereignty of his nation. Quoting the words of a good Cuban and friend, who despite having come to this country for disagreeing with the Cuban government is still an honorable person, I want to take advantage of this moment to pay tribute to the worthy Cubans who live here as well, and to refute, along the way, another of the lies spread by the prosecution regarding our feelings towards the Cuban community: "Those boys were convicted for the crime of dignity."

Over two years ago, I received a letter from my father, in which he said, among other things, that he hoped a jury would be found in which the values of Washington, Jefferson and Lincoln prevailed. It is shameful that he turned out to be wrong.

But I have not lost hope in the human race and its capacity to pursue those values. After all, I do not think that Washington, Jefferson and Lincoln themselves represented the majority during the era in which they left their mark on the history of this nation.

And as these three sordid years go down in history, and a mountain of arguments, motions and technicalities come to bury a story of blackmail, power abuse and the most absolute contempt for such a highly praised justice system, polished to a shine it never had, we will continue to appeal to those values, and to the American people's vocation for truth. And we will do so with all the patience, faith and courage that we draw from the crime of dignity.

Thank you very much.

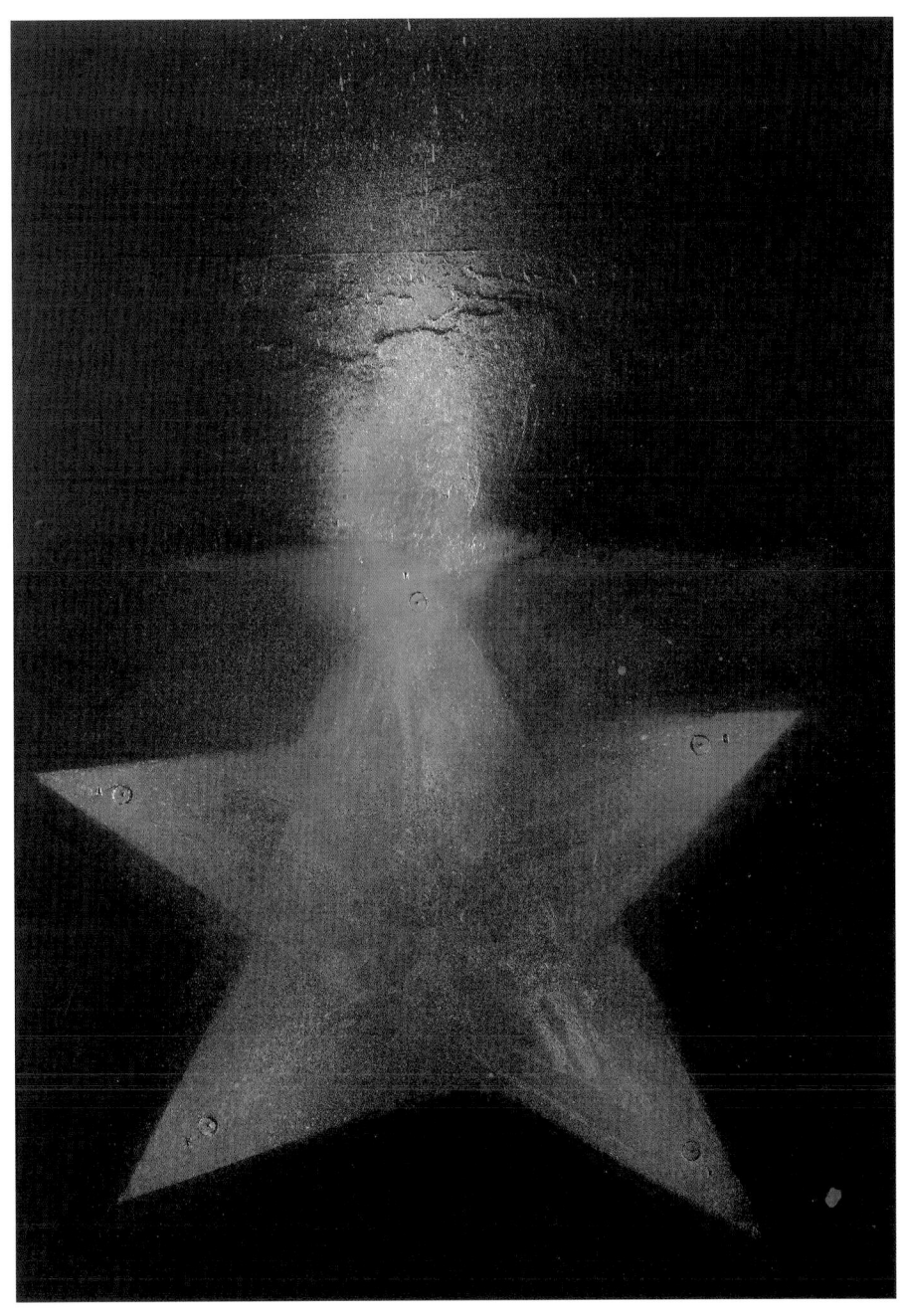

No tittle   MANUEL COMAS

Five years after our court statements

Now, five years after our sentences and Court statements, if we were to sum up that experience, we would have to say today that there is no substitute reading for those statements.

It could be said that the major difficulty at the time of drafting was to determine what should be left out, for lack of space. It was such a huge crime we had to denounce! There were so many truths to bring to light and so many reasons to defend! The Court statements were born and nourished from the trial and the six months that an unfathomable villainy cast its spell over that courtroom. They are full of justified rage, of much urgency and moral, because they fed on the Prosecution's lies that step by step contaminated everyone who was supposed to administer justice.

That mockery of a trial ended up as a conclave of deceit where every element of the judicial system competed to mislead it and the others. That entire murky environment gradually opened our eyes to face such a shocking perversity as could only come from a systemic disease. The unraveling of a fabric that could only result from a long established practice allowed us to look into the future where we encountered premonitions that have unfortunately been confirmed in the following five years.

The Court statements with their focus on the conflict and present validity are irreplaceable for the very content of their message at a time when the wounds are still fresh and it's urgent to tell the truth. That moment of our lives carried a unique intensity under circumstances that will never be repeated. All of this shows in our statements.

Five years have passed and the momentum and the moral intensity of that special moment are still with us, giving us heart and encouraging our resistance.

On the other hand, that final warning inspired in six months of experience has not lost its validity during the whole process. "This history of blackmails, abuse of power and absolute contempt for such a highly praised judicial system," is still buried under a mountain of arguments, motions and technicalities.

Our five Court statements continue to be an invaluable instrument to bring history to light.

René González Sehwerert
Marianna Federal Correction
December 2006

The outcry of eleven million… ALEJANDRO LEYVA

jesús orta ruiz
el indio naborí

final sentence

To the heroes, prisoners of the empire

If mid the machetes and torches of our strife
thirst for freedom gave birth to glorious fighters
now our battle of ideas brought to life
five brave men pursuing Peace themselves no slighters.

And among birds of prey they were no bandits,
they were no mean assassins or drug dealers,
but, facing showy gowns and humble habits,
tough diamond-hard patriots chasing killers.

The devious court has ruled against The Five,
they were sentenced to be in prison while alive;
but one day they shall be back home safe and sound

by history all absolved and full of bliss
each carrying a wide smile, a poem, a kiss
and thus will they live with privilege profound.

No tittle Adigio Benítez

alberto guerra naranjo

THE HOLE

The guard brought the prisoner to a halt right where the light ended. It was an order. He was just a prison guard discharging an order; that's apparently what he meant by putting his hand on the prisoner's shoulder before pushing him into the hole. The man, who had lost track of time during the interrogation, realized that he'd been pushed into the world of shadows. But he understood it better when the prison guard closed the door. It was absolute darkness; thus was his world now.

    The guard instead cleaned his sweat-drenched neck with a worn piece of cloth and surrendered the keys to another guard. "I'm too old for this work," he said to himself. On his way home, as usual, he tried to forget the prisoner; he whistled a song from his childhood days, looked at the palm trees on top of the hills, the birds flying around, and certain streams. "I'm old and tired," he repeated again to himself, as he tied the horse. Then, he smelled the food and felt hungry. He needed a good meal to forget the insults, the burning, the face- slapping, the piercing. "It smells good," he said to himself, as he walked to the shallow pan to wash. There, shirtless and leaning forward, in the same position as he had seen the prisoner held by others, he splashed water on his torso, much water, then he stopped, and with his two hands holding the rim of the shallow pan he looked at the native girls that were his property as they prepared the cassava; he saw the dog licking his boots, then the palm trees and the hills, but he couldn't forget the prisoner. He remembered the man screaming in fear as he walked to the house dripping water, much water.

The woman waited at the table; she always did. There was green beans stew, hard black bread, pork meat and papaya in syrup. The sweating fat woman, so different from the native girls outside, watched her husband eating like a beast.

"And, how is everything?" she asked. "As usual," he said.

"They say that a certain Guamá is burning the Encomiendas[1], killing innocent people and destroying everything he finds…"

"Who says that?" he retorted.

 "Everyone does."

"Hey, woman, don't you go around believing what everyone says."

"But that is what they say is happening."

"Nothing is happening, goddam it."

In the early morning hours the bed felt silent; there was another noise. It came from the window. The body of the prison guard got off the woman's body stretching an arm to take a sword to get up and face it. But it was not a native or any other man who made the noise; it was a bird.

The following day, still sleepy, the prison guard received from another guard the key to the hole. That strange bird perched on the window frame had not let him sleep. He had spent the night remembering its eyes, the strange way it flapped its wings, and how high it had flown to escape from him. The prisoner, however, was unaware of time. He lived in a world of darkness, that's why he screamed, his eyes hurting from the light, when the guard opened the door gap. He'd brought the man a plate of pigswill. The prisoner screamed and said something strange. "Mad, you're mad," said the guard as he shut the door gap. The desperate prisoner felt his way to the plate in the darkness; it was long since he had eaten. He brought the plate to his nose and felt nauseated but he stopped short of vomiting. He breathed deeply, he had to breathe deeply. Then he closed his eyes and devoured the pigswill as if it were a delicacy, or green beans stew, pork meat and papaya in syrup just cooked by a fat woman.

The prison guard, exhausted from the previous night, gave the keys to another guard and walked to the street. A 1956 Chevy almost hit him, so he headed for the sidewalk as somebody called him an asshole. He was sleepy. Besides, the prisoner's phrase kept drumming in his head. He was upset when he looked at the racing Chevy. He'd been called an asshole because he was dressed in plainclothes. It was different when he wore his uniform, he thought to himself, as he stood in front of a shop window. The suit fit him well, and the new tie, and the two-colored shoes; of course, unless he was called an asshole. He would buy a bottle of cider

---

[1] Encomiendas, land and natives granted to a colonist to work for him. (N. of the T.)

and run to the mulatto girl's house to forget the screaming, and also what the prisoner had said. He didn't have to pay for the cider; the owner of the grocery store near the police station was a good guy, he never charged, but the taxi cab he had to pay. He was no Ventura or Carratalá[2]; he was simply a guard. That's what he thought as he looked through the car window at the advertisements, the shop windows, the movie theaters, the lottery vendors and the pedestrians.

The mulatto girl watched him eating like a beast. There was black beans stew, white rice, fried plantain, pork steak and papaya in syrup.

"And, how is everything?" she asked. "As usual," he said.

"They say that the rebels are seizing the towns and that the government is falling apart…"

"Who says that?" he retorted.

"Everyone does."

"Hey, woman, don't you go around believing what everyone says."

"But that is what they say is happening."

"Nothing is happening, goddam it."

The guard was so upset that he pushed back his plate and walked to the window. He took out a cigar and lit it slowly, very slowly. Outside the house everything was quiet, orderly, nothing happened. "Nothing could happen," he thought. But, suddenly he remembered the prisoner, and what the prisoner had said. "Stupid lunatic," he thought, "it was stupid to say that he was a bird, that he was freer than me because he was a bird."

The following day, still upset, the guard walked down the street. He had felt so uncomfortable in bed that he didn't even care about the mulatto girl's body; her hot, naked body. He hadn't slept for a few days. "The country is upside down," he thought. One had better be careful. The city was boiling; the shouts of vendors, the whores, the petit thieves, the conspiracies and the conspirators. A mixture of good smells and bad smells at the street corners, the well-dressed youngsters and the people dressed in rags, the poor white and the poor black, the pretentious mulatto men and the arrogant black men. One has to be careful, foremost with the carriages, and with the smelly potholes. And also with those buckets of dirty water thrown from the doors without previous warning; and with the milkmen who disregard their cows; and with the black coachmen who try to get even taking their carriages through the street potholes full of dirty water, splashing, and dirtying everyone around. They fuck your life and there is nothing you can do about it. The owners hear the pedestrians protesting, show

---

[2] Ventura and Carratalá, two notorious senior Cuban policemen and assassins with Fulgencio Batista's force. They tortured and killed many young revolutionaries. (N. of the T.)

their heads out of the window and that's it, as if they agreed with the black coachmen.

The prison guard received the keys from another guard and sat down slowly. "I'm too old and tired for this work," he said to himself. It was almost time to retire. He fell asleep thinking he was no longer a prison guard, but he woke up to give the prisoner his ration of pigswill. "Goddam rebel," he thought, "bastard, the mother homeland is sacred." The guard stirred the stew and covered his nose. This food was not fit for any man. It was pigswill, prisoners' stuff. The food fit for a man could be a plate of chickpeas cooked by a woman, even if she was a fat mulatto woman. She would be watching him eating like a beast, after he came back from his job as a guard, and there would be cheese on the table, white bread, grape wine and love, much love. But the prison guard had no woman, only dreams, and he was terribly tired. He opened the door gap to the hole where the prisoner was and, as usual, he introduced the plate. He enjoyed watching the prisoner's hands feeling his way to the plate and sensing his nervous hands taking the pigswill to his mouth. He enjoyed it. However, it was different this time; the plate remained untouched.

"So you're not hungry today."

The prison guard leaned forward trying to look through the door gap. It was completely dark. For a few more minutes, he kept looking, but to no avail. Could he be dead? If he was dead, it was not his business. He didn't want any trouble. The man had died during the previous shift, certainly not on his watch, he thought. The prison guard whistled and soon there were other guards in front of the hole.

"Open up!" the chief said, and the door was opened. The lanterns brought light to the hole, but the prisoner wasn't there. The prison guard looked at the others in astonishment. He couldn't believe it. They wanted to get him involved in his escape. "I warn you, I'm not his accomplice," he screamed, but a strange noise held him back. It was a bird; the quick flapping of wings carrying it high, as high as it wanted, almost effortlessly.

Thursday, January 25, 2007

cintio vitier

rené

One would say the novel
of all hypocrisy
was your quilt writing
whole nights awake,
in that deep hole.

And now you come denouncing,
standing tall as a palm tree,
and the Light from your soul is so bright
in diamond you turn
the filthy hole.

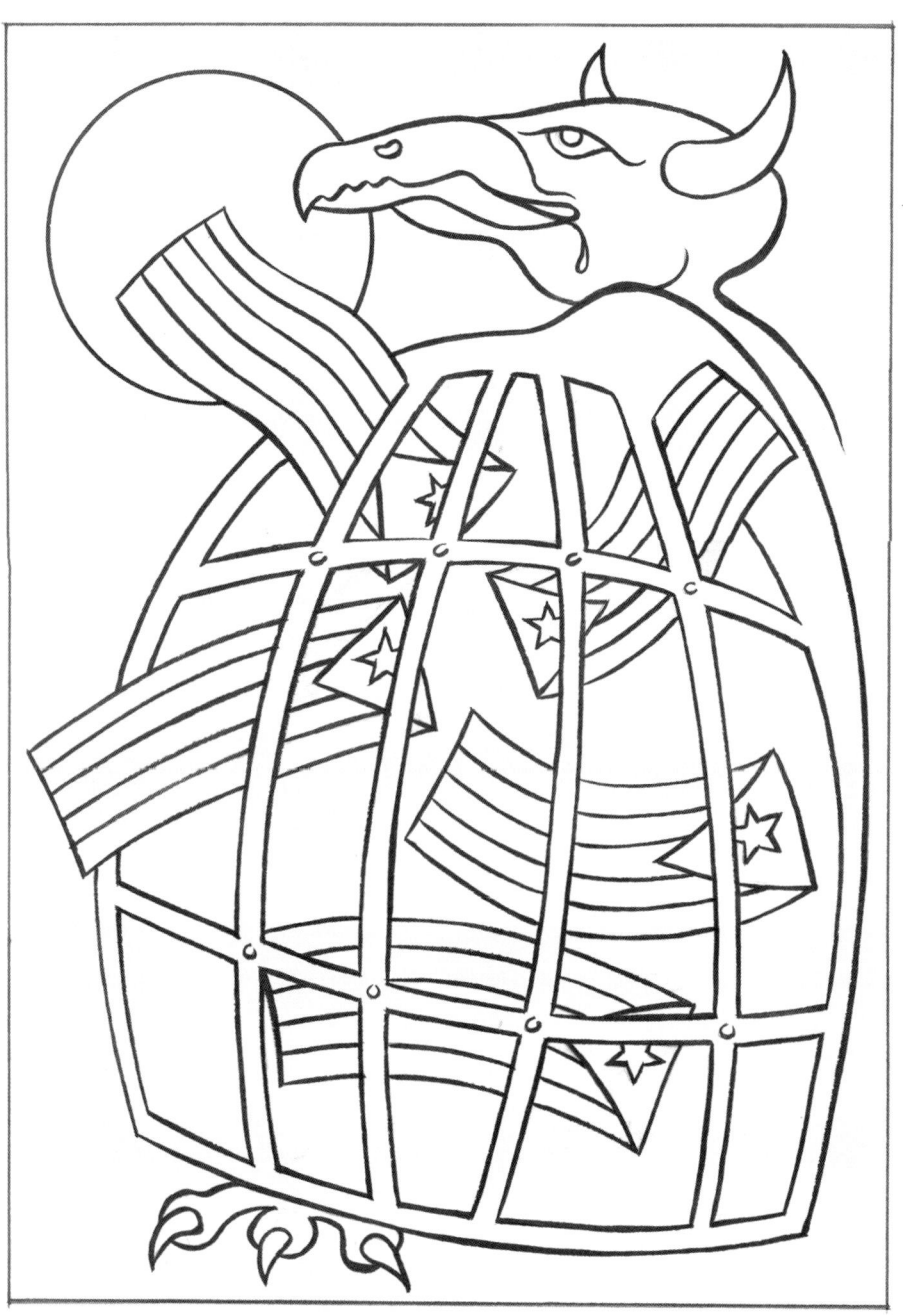

No tittle JUAN MOREIRA

The issue of the Five is such a scandal that it is difficult to speak about it.

Noam Chomsky
Outstanding American intellectual

The incarceration of the Five is one of the biggest legal scandals of the 21st Century. The European media are boycotting the case; the papers, radio and television would not deal with this story. This is a totally censored case.

Ignacio Ramonet
Editor of Le Monde Diplomatique

Nothing justifies that (the Five) are still in prison.

Wole Soyinka
Nobel Prize in Literature

*Never mind a sour bile of weakness
coming out rotten from a royal seed
nor would suffice all the world's vileness
to strangle our firm gentleness indeed.*

Fragment of a poem written by René to his parents

Try and be happy at all costs. Don't you allow yourself a pessimist thought or an unpleasant memory; don't you let the mark of a despicable action that once made you suffer get at you again. Keep in mind that you never gave in, neither inside or outside prison, and that you got over all this thanks to your strong nature, your morale and your principles.

Excerpts from one of Rene's letters to his wife

Meanwhile, we shall continue to be the owners of our laugh and optimism, of our joy for life and the satisfaction of having gone through all this without bending our knees, without taking humiliation, without yielding to blackmail and, above all, without bitterness.

If there is still anything I should say it is thank you for your love, for your support and for having stayed with me all this time giving me the encouragement that keeps me company and forever will.

To my dearest little baby:
At the time of my arrest, on September 12, 1998, you were hardly four and a half months old. The previous night your mother had gone to work and I stayed with you. When I gave you your bottle of milk you fell deeply asleep on my chest and I decided to let you stay while I remained quietly watching TV. When your mother came in she found it so funny that you were lying sprawled on your back with a sweet expression of satisfaction on your face that she couldn't help the temptation and took a picture of us.
THAT IS THE LAST PICTURE WHERE WE ARE TOGETHER

Nine years later he could again hold her against his chest

To Irmita in her sweet fifteen

*Fly away high, my butterfly. Go break spears
while you harvest your happiness and dreams
may the legacy of your sweet fifteen springs
be the gentle core which sprouts your universe
sound foundation of love to which this verse
we dedicate with pride. ¡And without fears!*

September 15th, 1999

YOU WILL NOT SEE A PICTURE OF OLGA SALANUEVA WITH RENE IN PRISON because the United States government, in a flagrant human rights violation, has repeatedly denied her a visa.

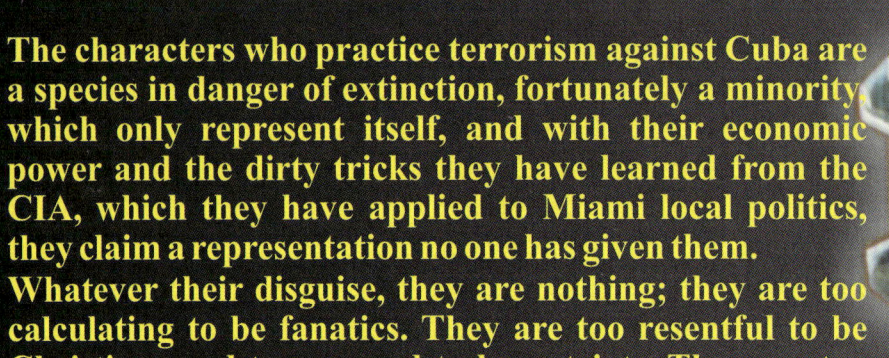

The characters who practice terrorism against Cuba are a species in danger of extinction, fortunately a minority, which only represent itself, and with their economic power and the dirty tricks they have learned from the CIA, which they have applied to Miami local politics, they claim a representation no one has given them.

Whatever their disguise, they are nothing; they are too calculating to be fanatics. They are too resentful to be Christians and too coward to be patriots. They are too full of hatred to be clever and too selfish to be democrats. They are too much in favor of Platt Ammendment to be Cubans.

They are like pathetic parasites sticking to the tail of an elephant thinking that they are its head while resisting to accept that the elephant only remembers the tail when it needs to get rid of the flies.

I firmly believe that you can be a Catholic and be a good person, that you can be a Jew and be a good person, that you can be a capitalist, a Moslem or a communist and be a good person; but there is nothing like a good person who's a terrorist. You must be sick to be a terrorist, as you must be sick to believe there is something like good terrorism.

René González Sehwerert

ROMA

MILAN

AFRICA

MEDIO ORIENTE

BUENOS AIRES

R. DOMINICANA

VENEZUELA

As a condition of his supervised release, the accused is prohibited from associating himself or visiting specific places known to harbor or be the haunts of individuals or groups such as terrorists.

Judge Lenard, during the sentences hearing, December 14, 2001

My only regret is that I have but one life to
give for my country.

GERARDO

daniel chavarría

THE 70-DEGREE RIGHT ANGLE

...and after only two weeks of recalling all the twisting and acrobatic positions the Tupamaro psychiatrist had to assume at the well-known Uruguayan prison of El Cilindro to survive inside a cube that measured 55.11 inches on the sides, your eighteen-square foot by six foot high 'hole' at the Miami prison seemed like a suite room in a five stars hotel; and suddenly you remember Edmund Dantes, surviving on his mere will thanks to the advice of abbot Faria who taught him to always keep his mind busy. That Tupa was a divine lunatic, and in the three lectures he gave in Havana, he came up as a professor of calamities, as a sportsman of survival. In the course of his lengthy flirting with death he had spent eleven years either hooded or shrinking in fear or being raped, as he said, but he never gave in, and once and again he came back from fainting in the torture chambers, excited because he had overcome new sufferings and set a new record against adversity like the masochistic climbers of the Himalaya; and with his emaciated face like a blue and blond Karamazov, the Tupa, his eyes feverishly bright, claimed his platitude that everything is relative and declared that with the resources of self-hypnosis that he used to teach, plus the memory of worst tortures sustained by other comrades or described in the *Handbook of Persuasion* used by the Yankees at the School of the Americas to train the continent's torturers, anyone could make any part of his body feel anesthetized at will; and you, to avoid thinking on the tragic alternative of torture, so much in vogue among the Yankees, decided that during the waking hours you would keep your mind dutifully collecting munitions useful for the future as an antidote against the waiting, the uncertainty, the madness brought on by inaction and by the thoughts moving adrift lacking a pre-arranged course or destination; you decided to improve your artistic skills. And during that first stage in "the hole", which lasted over a year, you devoted yourself to thinking of or drawing in the air hundreds of cartoons that you could not draw on paper while in jail "due to security reasons"; and you persisted in that strenuous exercise of your imagination, which you alternated with intensive gymnastic sessions, right until exhaustion invited a restoring sleep. And so the hours passed while you looked for a graphic line that would emphasize Bush's rodent expression; or Cheney's medieval-villain expression worthy of Bosco's hallucinated models; or Condolezza's countenance, with her half-closed eyelids showing her origins in the Kingdom of Shadows; and sometimes with the tip of your finger you traced on the floor the lines of a drawing that you later disliked so you used your hand to erase a certain angle; and in less that a year, just like the blind chess players, you were able to see every detail of all those images you had thought about, as if they had already been printed. And then, when you had over one-hundred of them in your memory file you decided one day to scoff at the very United States as a nation, from its birth, from the arrival of the first waves of *pilgrims*, founders of the Seven Colonies, until today; and thus you conceived the ambitious idea of producing a *soap comic*, that is, an endless soap opera in the form of a cartoon story that would explain to the Cuban children, and to your children when they are born, and to your grandchildren, why most of the American people are unaware of all the injustice and violence imposed on us by their governments in one and a half century, and why most believe that Cuba poses a threat to them. And to begin your cartoon story you thought of an incident that *si non é vero é ben trovato* to exemplify the sequence of *fear, ignorance, genocide and geophagy* that prevailed in the Seven Colonies' relations with their surroundings (and that has evolved until today's foreign policy shaped by a *Messianic superiority complex, ignorance, genocide and petrolphagy*), and you imagined an episode in the days when the Mayflower arrived in the territory of what is known today as New England, with one of those first groups of immigrants, and a denunciation that during the journey a young maiden had intercourse with a young sailor; and in fear that such sinful lust would invite the wrath of God against the new colony its brand-new authorities decided to hold a Thanksgiving service, and as a first act of government, to burn both suspects at the stake. But it happened that a group of messengers from the native population, the natural owners of that land, had come from a nearby encampment to the landing place. They had come in a parliamentary mood and to find out if the travelers could offer any favorable bartering, but when they saw the stakes where the condemned couple was burning, they stopped in amazement watching the victims writhing in agony amidst the flames; and the colonizing Puritans, scared by the sight of those darker men so different from them, promoted a swift and secret meeting of the town council whose leadership proclaimed that those visitors with their painted faces, their braids and loincloths could only be agents of the Unmentionable, and right then and there, after the pre-emptive lynching of the parliamentary entourage they pre-emptively killed every human being in the neighboring encampment, too; and in the mental script of your super-cartoon story the descendants of the Puritans from this colony, in alliance with their peers, the white Anglo-Saxon protestants from other towns, would first conquer the neighboring lands and later wide areas in Canada, the Mid West, Texas, Louisiana and California; and from the 18th century they would try to seize Cuba and the rest of the continent; and at the end you planned to leave some space to explain that in that great nation founded by very religious communities, instead of loving one another, they founded a society of *winners and losers* where being poor was disgraceful while they could easily forgive those who amassed large fortunes at gunpoint, as in the West, or through abuse and swindle; and after a few years, with a bit of makeup and charitable donations many crimes were forgotten; and this dichotomy of *winners and losers* has come to be regarded as the only code of conduct, the guide, the compass of ordinary Americans, who have long forgotten the Bible precepts of their ancestors when they believed that it was easier for a camel to go through the eye of a needle than for a rich man to enter the Kingdom of Heaven; and also an overwhelming majority finds unacceptable the Christian dictum of loving one another. Because, how could a decent, healthy, clean person love a *homeless*, smelly, filthy loser, who doesn't have a penny to pay for a roof and food, who's sick and sleeps on the streets under cardboard or newspapers? And one of the characters in your story could be pastor Robertson, a good friend of Reagan and Bush, Sr., a man who preaches on television to millions of fundamentalists of the extreme Christian right, and openly advises to murder Chavez; and you could have him explain that when Christ used the term "neighbor" he must have obviously been thinking of proximity, that is, someone near in terms of social classes; as for the camel, Robertson would argue that it was certainly an apocryphal excerpt because Christ could hold nothing against the honest rich who make up the driving force of every community, who create jobs, like Henry Ford, founder of charitable institutions, schools and hospitals, and Robertson would suspect that in the camel metaphor Christ condemned the "dishonest rich", but undoubtedly in the Old Ages one heretic or communist had removed from the Bible the term "dishonest"; and you must be specially careful when you address the Cuban children because that phrase of loving one another is quite a phrase, and any Cuban child or teenager or adult could call himself a patriot, a devotee of Fidel, a staunch anti-imperialist, but to admit that he cannot love just any neighbor, above all if the guy stinks, or if he has fleas and is also a drunk and a jerk…Thus your cartoons should explain that old Christian slogan, which according to Hugo Chavez can also be a communist slogan, a call from Jesus Christ to fight for the eradication of abject poverty and for the construction of a new beautiful homeland, one that is really optimistic, healthy and inclusive where one can really embrace any neighbor cleaned of fleas by the new society of justice, well-fed and learned. As for the camel, Christ surely condemns wealth and promotes an egalitarian, classless society. And, thus, thanks to you the Cuban children would be able to reflect some day and clearly see that the *wasp* (*white Anglo-Saxon Protestant*) families, which in the films never fail on the weekend religious rituals, do not believe in the true Christ or care about entering a Kingdom of Heavens that they would have to share with the world's poor. And then you decide that in your cartoon story you need to include Mr. Monroe, who, frightened by the interference of the Sacred Alliance, proclaimed his doctrine of "America for Americans", and from then on, the United States regarded the rest of the continent as their own backyard where they boycotted the works of patriots and supported the oligarchies and their obsequious tyrants, and if anyone had doubts let Sucre, Eloy Alfaro, Zapata, Sandino and many others speak for themselves; and after one and a half century of deceit and plundering of numerous peoples in the world, the citizens of the United States were finally convinced, at the end of World War II, that God had chosen them to impose democracy and freedom on Earth. To that end, God turned them into the mightiest military and economic power in history, and gave them such leaders as Harry Truman, the idiot, the smiling bomber of Hiroshima and Nagasaki who raised his hand with the V signal, the same that scared them off with the anti-communist terror of Mc Carthy who silenced the opponents of the American Way of Life, the likes of Dashiell Hammett and Charlie Chaplin, under threat of including them in the black list of enemies of democracy; and ever since then, marines and soldiers of that colossal nation in their holidays took to climbing the public monuments to urinate on the heads of the founding fathers of Latin America. And, it was their plan in the 1950s to turn the Caribbean, particularly Cuba, into a brothel, a gambling den and the stage for every injustice and violence directed by the Yankees and executed but their lackeys under Batista. BUT THEN HERE WAS FIDEL who resurrected Martí, yes Sir, and the Commander put an end to all of that, and you who were born in a family that loved José Martí, when you were old enough to understand the meaning of the Moncada, the fruitful imprisonment, the exile, the Granma, the Sierra, you who grew up loving your homeland and then in prison you once dreamed that you had escaped from your Yankee jail and come to Havana, walked up and down its streets, rolled on them, kissed its soil and that upon waking up from that dream you remembered that other bout of youthful patriotism that led you one day to the Revolution Square where before the statue of the Apostle you took a silent oath to always defend Socialist Cuba and Fidel, never to betray them, and it's precisely honoring that sacred love that you're preparing future cartoon stories that will keep your brain and nerves going and at the same time save you from alienation; and from day one you have fought to discipline yourself not to think too much about Adriana or about your loved ones who are so far away, or about the many happy moments spent together. And then, there is your faith in the inevitable return to your Homeland, based on what has been predicted by Fidel, that genie prophet, that man pampered by history, and pigeons, and orishas[1], that man who can foresee and outguess anyone; and there is also your certainty that the Yankees went too far in the trial against the Five, since their cynicism went as far as to consent that a Miami jury gave you *a life sentence* for your alleged complicity in the downing of two of Basulto's aircrafts, *a charge already dismissed by the Prosecution* for it was exhaustively proven false. Such a violation of the basic legal principle establishing the impossibility to condemn in the absence of proven charges excludes the United States of America from the community of democratic nations turning it into a sort of 1930's banana republic, the like of Tacho Somoza's Nicaragua or Papa Doc's Haiti, and also makes it the target of mockery, booing and Bronx cheers from any civilized law abiding society, because the same way it's impossible to construct buildings calculating 70-degree right angles, for they would crumble like the Twin Towers, the democratic states also fall apart when they shamelessly breach the legal alphabet, the basic principles enshrined in a Constitution, the international rules and norms and the common sense of ordinary people. And you're convinced that very soon the healthy and educated segment of the American people, plus international solidarity, will bring about a counter-reaction that will seek to wash the dirty laundry of the past administrations; and even such scoundrels as pastor Robertson and Cheeny will rather release the Five than face the daily demonstrations in front of the White House and Capitol Hill headed by Gloria de la Riva and thousands of Cindy Sheehans, the American version of Hebe de Bonafini and her Mothers of Plaza de Mayo. And you, Gerardo, you are confident that if not this year, it'll be the next, or the following year but the Pentagon and the White House gang of democracy-thieves and oil-pirates will realize that pleasing the Miami anti-Cuba Mafia is not a good reason to let the world see them like baloney and to cease being the Human Rights' leaders in Geneva and in their rigged summits for freedom, democracy and

---

[1] Orishas; name given to deities in African animist religions. (N.of the T.)

other such stories. Also, after eight years putting up with adversity, doing mental gymnastics, fighting earnestly against insanity, against time, memory, sadness and nothingness you have become one of the Five, a hero of world dimension, a personal triumph you never dreamed of, and sustained by your increasing love for your Homeland, for your loved ones, you're proud to be imprisoned in that hole for defending the most dignified nation in the world, the only one that sent 300,000 of its best sons and daughters to remove apartheid from Africa without asking for or receiving anything in return; the only country blockaded and assaulted that never abandoned the children from Chernobil and more than twenty years later, still blockaded and fucked up by the Yankees, by the hurricanes and the draughts it assigns medications, equipment, oncologists, specialized nurses and resources to care for hundreds of cases, while the humanitarian Europe, signatory to all sorts of manifestos in favor of all sorts of freedoms and rights, after offering aid and promising Heaven and Earth started to backpedal and didn't move a finger in favor of the thousands of Ukrainian children contaminated by radioactivity; and you're proud of being in prison for defending your Cuba, the same that today continues to heal and to educate the poor people of this world in Latin America, Africa and the Himalaya, the same that has helped thousands of helpless people to recover their vision without charging them a penny; the same that sets up schools and hospitals in Haiti and in Africa, and welcomes in its own territory thousands of youths from the Third World to train them as sport instructors, engineers, teachers and physicians who will one day work in their respective countries. Finally, you're proud to be unconditionally at the service of Fidel who has never bent his knees before the despots nor has he ever silenced an injustice, and when you are eventually out from your latest stay in "the hole" and you're allowed to make a phone call to your embassy and somebody there ask who you are, you'll laugh and think of a cartoon depicting you dressed in rags, paler and more bearded than you're now, and you'll answer, "It's the Count of Montecristo."

We shall be like Che JAVIER GUERRA

Defense statement presented by Gerardo Hernández Nordelo at the sentencing hearing held wednesday, december 12, 2001

Your Honor:

I would like first of all to express a few words of thanks to a number of federal government officials who worked throughout our long and complex trial both inside and outside this courtroom. I am referring to the translators, stenographers, marshals and other assistants, who showed a high professional ethic at all times.

I would also like to publicly express our deepest gratitude to the attorneys who so masterfully represented us, and to all of the people who assisted them in this very difficult task.

So as not to waste your valuable time, I will try to be as brief as possible. There are five defendants in this case, and we share many opinions and views, so I will refrain from referring to important aspects that I know they will want to address in their turn.

Moreover, it would take too much time to point out every one of the inconsistencies of the prosecution and its witnesses, every one of its efforts to use and sometimes manipulate small portions of the evidence while disregarding its larger and more essential significance.

The few minutes I have would not be enough to highlight all of the attempts made by the gentlemen of the prosecution to ensure that the jury was guided more by emotions and prejudices than by the facts and the law; nor would there be enough time to point out every one of the reasons that made this an eminently political trial.

Moreover, it might not even be necessary, because no one knows better than you what really happened in this courtroom between December 2000 and June 2001. Nevertheless, there are a number of elements that must not be overlooked.

Those who are not aware of the way the most radical sector of the Cuban community in Miami traditionally operates, those who do not watch Spanish-language television or listen to so-called "Cuban radio", might have sincerely thought that it would be possible for us to be given a fair and impartial trial in this city. Unfortunately, there are many realities of which the U.S. public is still unaware. As for us, from the very moment that we were denied the possibility of having the trial moved out of Miami, we did not have the slightest doubt of what the final outcome would be.

It would be dishonest to deny that as the trial progressed, and in view of the overwhelming arguments and evidence put forward by the defense, combined with the frequently desperate behavior of the prosecution and the reaction of the press, there were moments when we even considered that what seemed to be impossible in this community could perhaps really happen. Yet the jury, with its quick and unequivocal verdict, proved our initial prediction to be accurate. After six months of a complex and exhausting trial, with dozens of testimonies and extensive evidence, the members of the jury needed only a few hours, without even asking a question or voicing a doubt, to reach a unanimous verdict.

It is sufficient to read the statements made to the press by the spokesman of this jury to understand that we never had the slightest chance, and that they were influenced more by prejudices or by the final, deceptive words of the gentlemen of the prosecution than by the arguments they heard here over the course of half a year.

And when I refer to the deceptive behavior of prosecution, I am not making a disrespectful or unfounded accusation. As I said before, there is not enough time to point out every single example. It is enough to recall that the person responsible for translating the majority of the evidence used by the prosecution, an individual who claimed to be an expert in the field, stated before this court that the Spanish word "plastilina" is used to refer to plastic explosives, when in fact, any Hispanic child knows, without being an expert, that the only "plastilina" in our language is what is known in English as "molden clay". Incidentally, the prosecution used the document referring to this "plastilina" over and over again for its alarmist effect, despite knowing, because they do know, that it has nothing to do with any one of the five accused.

It is equally ridiculous that during the trial of people accused of being dangerous spies and a menace to national security, the accusing party has repeatedly stressed an incident that purportedly took place in Cuba, involving a taxi driver from the country's main airport, at a time when the island had just suffered a wave of terrorist attacks. I wonder how many taxi drivers are being watched by the FBI at this very moment in airports across the United States, not only for expressing their discontent with the government, but probably simply for wearing turbans. In order to understand the attitudes of a country or its citizens, it is necessary to live, or suffer, its daily realities. The above-mentioned incident, as inconceivable as it may seem, was even included in the PSI report, although no one could explain what relation it might possibly have to the crimes I have been accused of.

Now that I have mentioned the PSI report, I would like to briefly refer to some of the statements I wrote for the same, and I quote: "Cuba has the right to defend itself from the terrorist acts that are prepared in Florida with total impunity, despite the fact that they have been consistently denounced by the Cuban authorities. This is the same right that the United States has to try to neutralize the plans of terrorist Osama Bin Laden's organization, which has caused so much damage to this country and threatens to continue doing so. I am certain that the sons and daughters of this country who are carrying out this mission are considered patriots, and their objective is not that of threatening the national security of any of the countries where these people are being sheltered." End of quote.

This statement was written for the PSI report and sent to my attorney to be translated many days before the tragic and condemnable events of September 11. Today they are more relevant than ever. Just as the president of the United States stated recently before the United Nations, it is necessary for all of the world's countries to unite in the struggle against terrorists, and not against some terrorists, but rather against all terrorists. And I would add that as long as the acts of some of these criminals are condemned, while others are sheltered and allowed to act with impunity against the security and sovereignty of other countries, and considered "freedom fighters", this scourge will never be eradicated. And as long as this is the case, there will always be nations that need to send some of their own people to carry out dangerous missions for their defense, whether it be in Afghanistan or South Florida.

Your Honor, we have been accused of conspiring to commit espionage and harm the national security of the United States. We have been placed on the same level as the worst spies ever known, without a single piece of sound evidence and without having caused any harm whatsoever, solely on the basis of suppositions. Ours may be one of the most ridiculous accusations of espionage in the history of this country. Everything that we intended to do and have done was clearly set out in the evidence put forward. The person who was closest to anything military, after six years of working in his insignificant post, was merely asked to try to find a position that allowed him to be closer to the runways, in order to observe the number of planes. This is not espionage. The evidence and testimony offered by individuals highly qualified in this area have demonstrated that.

On the other hand, it is true that for years, some of we the accused had false identity documents in our possession, but their only purpose was to guarantee our safety. As a judge, you are aware of how many crimes can be committed with false documents, and yet it was acknowledged in this courtroom that the only use made of these documents, when they were used in any way at all, was exclusively aimed at protecting our own personal integrity and that of our families.

Please permit me to briefly refer to what I believe is the reason for which all of us find ourselves here at this moment: the third in the list of charges against us, "conspiracy to commit murder".

The prosecutors and FBI authorities know and knew from the very beginning what truly did take place before, on and after February 24, 1996. They themselves had to acknowledge that the high frequency messages they chose to reveal as evidence are only a minute portion of all the messages they intercepted. They know the true story. They know that there was never any conspiracy to shoot down those planes, much less to do it over international waters. They know perfectly well that not only Gerardo Hernández, but also not even Juan Pablo Roque ever had anything to do with a plot to shoot down the planes. They know that Roque's return had been planned long before for strictly personal reasons, and that in February of 1996, instructions were given for he himself to choose his date of departure, with the recommendation that it be either February 23 or 27, depending upon the availability of airline tickets. If there had been a plot in which Roque was involved, how could he have stayed here until the 27th? This is just one of the many details that make this the most absurd and outrageous of all the charges against us.

After two years of close surveillance, and having taped most of our telephone and personal conversations and confiscated a large quantity of materials from that time period, the prosecutors could not present a single piece of evidence at this trial to demonstrate beyond reasonable doubt that Gerardo Hernández had conspired to shoot down these planes or contributed in a way to this act. They based their entire case on pure speculation, on small excerpts of documents, manipulated and taken out of context, and above all on the emotional and sensitive nature of this accusation, due to the loss of human lives.

It would only be natural to ask what motivated the prosecution to stage its whole propaganda show around this charge, and to seek at any cost to convict someone who they know had nothing to do with the death of those people. The answer is not all that difficult to find. One need only recall the enormous pressure exerted by some sectors of the Cuban community who were not satisfied with the economic sanctions adopted against Cuba following the events of February 24. The repeated accusations made by these individuals and organizations against the government of the United States for its alleged complicity in these events, according to them, and for not doing anything to punish those responsible, became ever more bothersome, just as it was bothersome and unforgivable to these Miami Cubans that the FBI regional office would have infiltrated informers into a number of so-called "exile" organizations, including the "Brothers to the Rescue". It had become necessary to restore images and improve relations, and nothing would work better than finding, or fabricating, a guilty party.

The authorities knew this was a win-win situation. If I was found guilty of the charge, all the better. If I was found innocent, as unlikely as that may have seemed, they would still win, because they could silence those who were accusing them of not having charged anyone.

Perhaps there are people so naive or unaware as to believe that I am exaggerating the importance that some U.S. authorities accord to the opinions and reactions of the most extremist sector of the Cuban community. I would like to remind those people of the fact that the citizens of this nation cannot travel freely to Cuba, or smoke Cuban cigars, or trade in Cuban products without restrictions, or simply immunize their children against diseases for which the only vaccines are patented in Cuba, and further remind them that this fact does not exactly respond to the demands or interests of the American people.

Your Honor, I have always said, and will repeat now, that I deeply regret the loss of those four lives, and I understand the suffering of their families. I also regret the thousands of lives that have been lost as a result of the constant aggression suffered by my people throughout more than 40 years, and the eternal mourning of many, many Cuban families. These dead also have names and faces, although their pictures cannot be shown in this courtroom.

Cuba did not provoke this incident. On the contrary, it foresaw it, and tried to prevent it through every means within its reach. The prosecution's main argument during the trial was that this incident was a crime, because it involved unarmed civilian aircraft. This nation recently found out, in an unfortunate and brutal manner, just how much damage can be done to its people by an unarmed civilian plane. Perhaps that is why its top leaders have warned that any plane that strays threateningly from its scheduled route should be shot down, even if there are hundreds of passengers on board. Perhaps the gentlemen of the prosecution believe this would be a crime. Your Honor said today that this country changed its "perception of danger" after September 11; unfortunately, Cuba had to change its perception of danger on January 1, 1959, and this is what some people fail to understand.

The people primarily responsible for what happened on February 24, 1996 are the same people who do not relent in their efforts to provoke an armed conflict between the United States and Cuba, so that this country's army can do for them what they themselves have not managed to do in 40 years. Be it flotillas, airspace violations, false accusations or any other abomination, the goal is always the same: for the United States to wipe the Cuban government and those who support it off the face of the earth, no matter what the cost in human lives on one side or the other. It can be stated with all certainty that if anyone has repeatedly placed the national security of this country in danger, it has been these extremist Cuban groups.

The prosecution stated in this courtroom, during the final arguments, that Gerardo Hernández has blood on his hands. I wonder whose hands really are stained with blood, if it is me, or the individual who fired a gun on a hotel full of people in Havana, who is the same individual who appears in the evidence of this case planning to smuggle antipersonnel weapons into Cuba; the same person who openly and recklessly defied the Cuban authorities, over and over and over again, violating the laws of that country, the laws of this country, and the most elemental rules of international aviation; the same person who not only did not hesitate to lead these young men to their deaths, but who also, in the moments of greatest tension, when there was still time to go back on his plans, did not do so, and instead left his laughter on tape for all of history, while his comrades were dying.

This person's hands truly are stained with blood, yet this did not seem to matter to the gentlemen of the prosecution when they shook those bloodied hands on numerous occasions, even in this very courtroom. Nor did it matter to the prosecutors or the top FBI authorities in Miami when they shared the stage and the celebrations with this same person during the press conference on the day the verdict was announced. This is rather contradictory behavior for those who claim to represent the law.

I want the gentlemen of the prosecution to know that the only blood there may be on these hands is the blood of my brothers and sisters who have fallen or been cowardly murdered in the countless acts of aggression and terrorism perpetrated against my country by individuals who freely walk the streets of this city today. And it is for this blood that I made the pledge to sacrifice even my own life if doing so could protect my people from such crimes.

Your Honor, the prosecution considers, and has requested, that I should spend the rest of my life in prison. I trust that if not at this level, then at some other level of the system, reason and justice will prevail over political prejudices and the desire for revenge, and it will be understood that we have done no harm to this country that deserves such a punishment. But if this were not the case, I would then take the liberty of quoting one of this nation's greatest patriots, Nathan Hale, when he said: "My only regret is that I have but one life to give for my country."

Thank you very much.

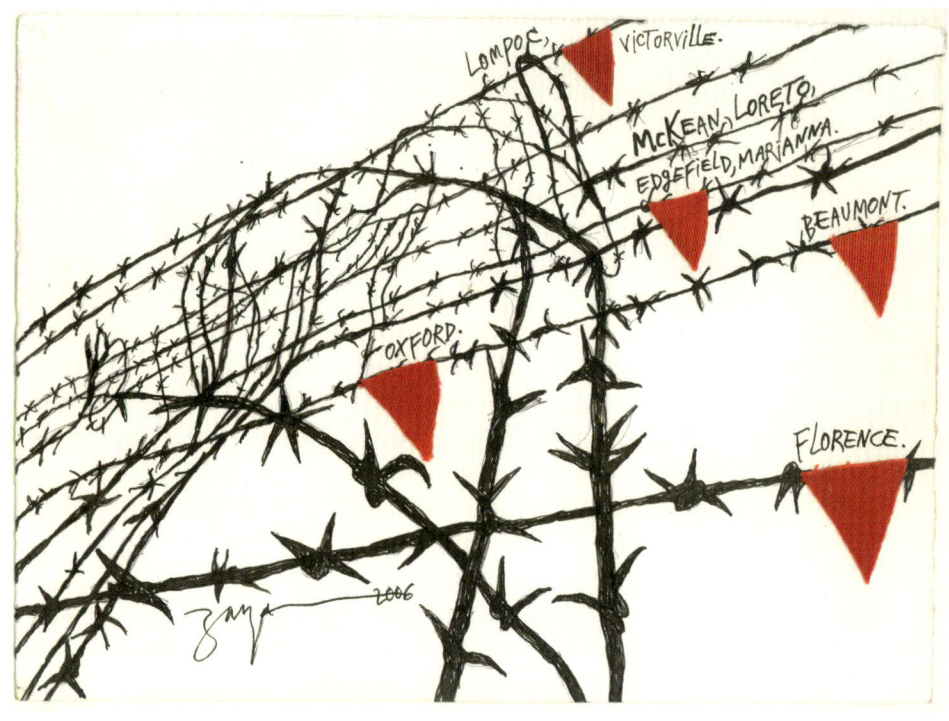

No tittle   RAFAEL ZARZA

Five years after our court statements

That December 12, when I turned on the radio and heard the strident Ninoska Pérez Castellón, spokesperson of the anti-Cuban Miami Mafia, I had no doubt that my court statement had hit a nerve. "He is a cynic!" she repeated again and again, as she gave her listeners her own version of what had happened in Court. "Why didn't he use one his Commander's phrases instead of quoting one this country's patriots? He is a cynic…!"

Ninoska had been in the courtroom with José Basulto and other such characters. They could not miss the show; after so many failures it was finally their chance to score one point "against Castro." It's true that everything in the trial had gone wrong and that they had turned from accusers into the accused, but that was meaningless now. The final moment was close and the judge would pronounce sentence; that would be the real "show." They expected to see "Castro's spies" pleading for clemency. After all, isn't it what defendants do before they are read their sentence, that is, begging the Judge to be merciful, showing they are repentant and begging everyone present their forgiveness? According to Ninoska and her cronies, that should have been the script, but again they miscalculated the sentence hearing like they had miscalculated the trial.

Again, the representatives of the terrorist Mafia were victims of their traditional arrogance for they failed to take into account the dignity of the defendants' families and friends who took their seats in the same courtroom and, with their heads up high, represented all of our people telling us with their eyes, "You're not alone, we're here with you!" They failed to consider the "foolishness" of five men who, like many other Cubans, chose to have a place in their people's heart rather than "a corner on the altars" of those who have brought so much pain to our homeland.

I did not have the privilege of listening to my brothers' statements in court; I wasn't allowed to, but I have read them many times, and I know that during those four hearings all of the Ninoskas and all of the Basultos must have been sizzling, while they helplessly put up with the truths said right to their faces by Ramón, Fernando, Antonio and René, who never showed the slightest sign of fear or repentance.

Unfortunately, the vast majority of people in Miami don't have any idea of what happened in that trial nor what we said in our statements, because the famous "sun city" is really a city of darkness, and it won't cease to be so while the mainstream media, like most of the agencies, are controlled by the same anti-Cuban Mafia that prevented us from having a fair trial.

Five years later justice has not been served and our statements are so relevant that they could be repeated today.

Five years later, some of these characters whose craving for vengeance was apparently not satiated are still hopeful; they don't understand. Meanwhile, certain newspaper reproduces speculations from "anonymous sources" which dream that time and the rigors of prison will have their impact and any of the "fools" may give in.

That's why, five years later it would be worthwhile doing as Ninoska asked; she was so upset that in my statement I did not use any of our Commander-in-Chief's phrases that after eight years of unjust imprisonment, there is one phrase I would add today, in capital letters:

HOMELAND OR DEATH! WE SHALL OVERCOME!

Gerardo Hernández Nordelo
Victorville Federal Prison
California, January 2007

Light   EDUARDO ROCA SALAZAR (CHOCO)

césar lópez

warning

> *Against those who want to rule the world*
> *but live outside the rules*
>
> *...since, immersed in a wounding restlessness,*
> *you do not wish to correct yourself, but you*
> *dare to correct the earth and sky.*
>
> FRANCISCO DE QUEVEDO[1].

After a time, as if they had ever
calmed down, they went back to their inexcusable criminal intrigues,
although always hiding behind crass laws, showy prayers, nonsense.

And there they are again! Humiliating,
confining, forgetting, if by chance they were ever aware of it,
the dignity of man, of women, of all creatures…
When bells toll or angels sing
it is to hide the hypocrisy of the veiled imperial speeches.
How can ignominy pass unnoticed
when prison doors remain locked
and the mere resistance involves risking life
in addition to vulgar condemning demonstrations.

---

[1] Contra los que quieren gobernar el mundo
 Y viven sin gobierno
 ...pues, ocupado en un mordaz desvelo,
 a ti no quieres enmendarte, y osas
 enmendar en el mundo tierra y cielo.
  Francisco de Quevedo

And we are not talking, silence,
about academic formalities
or manipulated laws,
you can hear the trumpets, as they repeat
references to convenient wars, deceitful roles,
some men feel insulted while murderers
are not even sorry because they were never clean
and insist on recruiting slaves. When are you planning
to change your ways, gentlemen! Or should we call you beasts?
Out of the labyrinth. Monsterlike people. Gates
will no longer be closed and the widest
path shall lead to life. They ought to know that right now.
Decency is meant to star in history.
It is never too late. *Let the woodcutter awake!*[2]
If he doesn't, the children of the Earth will.

The cruel and unfair punishment
our brothers' suffering should be lifted.
May justice be applied justly if it really exists:
Justly; stop the lies and tricks that grow old
before salvation. *The universe speaks better than humankind*[3]
but humanity should not remain silent today. We must talk
with that voice that demands freedom, the full
independence of the act. The supreme mission. To hold on
to life. Stay not still in the face of crime
prolonged there in isolated dungeons while the world suffers torture,
wars, starvation, infamy, uncountable offences.
The constant threat of provoked death: No more!
Since you are the cause of terror: stop incriminating others!

Listen again Yankees![4] You won't make them surrender.

Havana, 2007.

---

[2] ¡Qué despierte el leñador!
                       Pablo Neruda
[3] El universo habla mejor que el hombre.
                                José Martí
[4] Title of the book by C.R. Mills

…*where men are born…* ERNESTO RANCAÑO

mylene fernández pintado

*To Gerardo, Ramón, René, Fernando and Antonio
who are the inspiration.*

THE WORLD, MIDDLE AGES

On March 8 of the year 2000, Pope Wojtyla made his petition of pardon for all the harm that for centuries the Church had brought on humanity. As he was reciting his *mea culpa*, John Paul II was especially thinking of the victims of the Holy Inquisition, the proceedings of the Middle Ages Tribunal which for centuries persecuted, tortured and condemned hundreds of thousands of people to burning at the stake.

We, by Divine Mercy Inquisitor General, with full confidence in your discretion and zeal for the faith, we appoint you, create you, and constitute you Apostolic Inquisitors against heretical iniquity and apostasy in the inquisition of…

The man is smiling. He congratulates himself on his good memory for he remembers the formula invariably recited to the inquisitors at the moment of investiture. He has decided to include it in the book, literally. But the point at which he has interrupted the phrase calls for a clarification.

…and apostasy in the inquisition of (and here the name was inserted of the place where the inquisitor was deputized)

Having made the clarification the quotation goes on:

>...giving and granting you entire authority to make inquiries on every person, man or woman, dead or alive, absent or present, of any state or condition, who might be guilty, suspicious or accused of the crime of apostasy and heresy, and above every other framer, pleader or patron of the same.

The man tries to remember many other things for his book, like the fact that the Inquisition was a Roman procedure of doubtful origin.

Then he writes that *"The Inquisition is based on an accusation brought on by the legal authorities, even in the absence of denunciations made by reliable witnesses. It grew strong at the end of the 12th century, and with the Ad Extirpandas papal bull of Innocent IV...*

He relishes the term *Extirpandas* feeling the horror of extirpating the souls and thoughts of people whose lives are taken because they are an inconvenience to those who always put out candles, and close down doors and windows; those who need darkness, the lords of Darkness.

>*...it is established that heresy is a State reason, and that torture is to be used to obtain confessions; that sinners are not only those who undermine the religious precepts but also the policies.*

The man is convinced that wars, repression and violence have always had the same purpose: wealth. That both the Crusades that massacred and destroyed Constantinople and the evangelization of the New World, as well as the expulsion and murder of Jews through the Alhambra Decree have engrossed the coffers of the powerful. And it's no surprise that the Inquisition decreed, a few years later, to have the heretics' property confiscated; they lacked the funds to sustain the institution.

>*The appointment of Friar Tomas de Torquemada as Inquisitor General of the kingdom of Castile and Aragon on October 1843, marked the beginning of the Modern Inquisition. The empire is large and powerful and the Inquisitorial Tribunal is an instrument to control it and a collaborator to sustain it and reinforce it. Torquemada establishes in the Capitulations that the punishments include the confiscation of the properties of those suspicious of heresy.*

Ah, so many abuses, the man thinks and he recalls Sixtus IV who deeply alarmed appealed to the Catholic Kings because the Inquisition had for some time been acting not out of zealousness or for the salvation of the souls but out of greediness, and even in the absence of any proof many people had ended up in secular prisons, tortured and condemned for heresy, collapsed and handed over to the secular authorities for execution. In its ambition, the empire has activated the Holy Office to confiscate properties and collect revenues. No eating without burning, thinks the man as a joke, and even though the phrase sounds somewhat shallow, he decides to include it. He remembers everything that the flames have devoured all these years. And we are still in the dark, he concludes.

He then describes the functioning of the Inquisitions.

The denunciations are anonymous. The prisoners are not confronted with the accuser or informer.

Especial provisions are issued to secure the secrecy of the proceedings and the anonymity of the witnesses.

Frequently there are false denunciations for proving an excessive zealousness and for other equally mean motivations.

The Inquisition creates an atmosphere where fear and distrust prevail among the people.

Everybody is fearful of others, the man thinks nodding sadly, and they prefer to see injustice prevail rather than be considered heretic. Being a suspect is tantamount to being guilty.

Although it is established that first the heresy should be qualified, some have been in prison for years waiting for their cases to be examined.

Time is of no consequence to the "qualifiers", he mutters. It's only the prisoner who establishes a special relationship with time, with every grave instant that stops escorted by others; with the past, which insists on devouring an almost motionless present; and, with every minute of the future which announces itself and parades before him for sixty seconds in the present to then go engross the past. It's the time he spends alone, in the dark and in silence. It's the time that is an orphan of nights and days, of voices and gestures.

The proceedings take place in the most absolute secrecy both for the public and the accused, who is not informed of the accusations brought against him. It could be that months and years pass and he is not informed of the reasons for his incarceration. He is kept in isolation and some die in prison.

It is for this reason that the man is writing his book, because silence is an allied of fear and because ignorance deprives people of their freedom. The flame must be used to shed light and not to reduce words to ashes and submerge everything in coldness and darkness.

In order to question the prisoner, the Inquisition resorts to torture to bring truth to light, *to exact confessions. Torturing is applied indistinctively of age, both to children and the old.*

Torturing is intended to cause pain, to bring suffering and degradation on another human being. It turns one person into the executioner of another person. The humiliation of the object of torture is more denigrating to his torturer. What goes through the mind of a torturer while his hand is tormenting those who could be his own family or neighbors? What is the dark side of humanity that is unleashed to take agony, screams and death to another human being placed in a totally helpless position? He wonders.

The man moves from his position. Ever since he decided to write the book, he has been devoting all his time to that. He has a lot of material and he needs to organize it, from the beginning of the proceedings up to the issuing of the sentences.

Acquittal is contemplated as one of the results of the proceedings but it hardly ever happens.
There is also the possibility of suspending the proceedings, of leaving the accused free but under threat that his process may be resumed at any time.
The accused can be punished and serve long terms in jail or in the galleys, or he can be lashed and his properties confiscated.
The accused can be condemned to punishment by the secular authorities, which implies death by burning at the stake. If the prisoner is repentant, he may be garroted before giving his body up to the flames. If not, he is burned alive. The act of execution is public.

The denunciation is anonymous, the proceedings are secret, and the execution is public. There is ignorance and silence; repression and fear. I am not a man of thoughts, he tells himself; I am just somebody who thinks. One of those who want to put an end to ignorance and silence, to exorcise fear, he tells himself once an again as he goes through his notes.

Among the charges foreseen by the Holy Office are those raised by the kindred. These are the lay servants who cooperate with the church officials. They take part in searches and arrests. They have many advantages: they enjoy fiscal benefits and jurisdictional privileges; they can only be judged by the Inquisition. And they are allowed to carry weapons.

These are the power beggars, the weak of spirit, the poor of soul; these are the ones that receive alms for playing the game of the powerful and are happy with the remains and with feeling feared; they gloat over being feared which they take for being respected. They are the lackeys of Evil; the man is angered by the memory of these. There will be a Final Judgment, he promises himself.

The inquisitorial institutions are seldom investigated even if their reprehensible conduct stained by improprieties is there for everyone to see.

Some have abjured, and the man waves his hair away from his eyes as if this would help him to better recall the abjuration speeches. It's not important to mention any, he thinks. Suffice it to say that he who abjures can also be given a penance. He must swear that he will denounce others. His life has been spared so that he will carry the penitent gown, be exiled or sent to the galleys, where he will probably find death.

The man has written a lot; he hopes he did not forget any details. He hopes that those who read his book find some answers to their questions but above all many more questions. Then he writes the last phrase, a query:

We are still without an explanation for the widespread use of violence, and for the ruthless and gratuitous humiliation of a human being; for this loss of a sense of reality on behalf of a hallucinating idea that brings death.

Finally, he should write down the date and place where the book was born, for he doesn't know when or where it will be published.

He adds:

"The World, Middle Ages"

The prisoner goes through the pages of his imaginary book, written with his recollections and the reflections in his memory. The darkness that surrounds him is the same whether his eyes are opened or closed, any time of day or night, which have ended up as an eternal moment suspended in the darkness.

Sitting against the stone wall, he stretches his arms and legs, and this movement is enough to recognize the other three walls that make up his cell. He has learned to recognize every crack of the wall, and its bumpy texture, from the touch of his hands.

With his eyes closed, he observes the dark and silent wall before him. Then, he discovers an inexistent window and a shaft of light coming through, and he smiles with the certainty that, finally, it's dawn.

Montagnola, Switzerland, April 2007[1]

---

[1] With appreciation to Paolo who almost wrote it with me.

cintio vitier

gerardo

Your look, gleammer
of your confident smile,
announced the summit
where manliness matures.

We see you now clamoring
herald of dignity
as before you were draftman
of farse and evilness.

But always up,
and always smiling,
looking forward in the distance

to the promising dawn at the end:
teh steady wise mother country:
noble, not arrogant.

No tittle JUAN MOREIRA

The case of the Cuban Five imprisoned in the United States remains a secret for the American people. History is not published in this country's newspapers. You don't hear anything about them... It's a violation not only of constitutional rights but also of human rights.

Howard Zinn, prestigious American intellectual

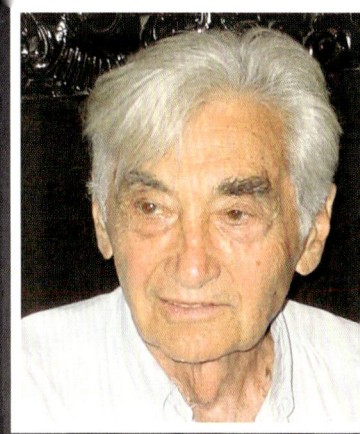

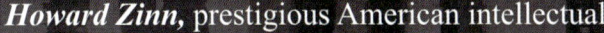

The case of the Five is additional evidence that we are experiencing a legal crisis, a political crisis and a constitutional crisis.

Gore Vidal, an American novelist, essayist and playwright

I urge that these men be returned to their homes and lives in Cuba.

Nadine Gordimer, Nobel Prize in Literature in a letter to *The New York Times* on April 11, 2003

These men [...] are proving something extraordinary that the rest of us should not ignore: that to go on loving deeply and tenderly honors the greatest achievements of the Revolution.

Alice Walker, 1982 Pulitzer Prize

Desire

*I'll tell you how deeply I appreciate your sleeplessness,
your infinite silence and your immense valor,
and you'll know how I long to return to the peerlessness
of your land, to be reborn in your arms and feel your ardor.
It will get to you in tears of passion and delight,
for hidden in my chest my return I'll await,
and how dearly I would love, during this long night,
for you to read these verses which to you I dedicate.*

Fragment of the poem Gerardo wrote to his mother while he was in "the hole"

…no memory hurts me more today and no image is bitterer than that of a tear running down your face. I also hurt for those tears that I have caused and not seen and I'm sorry […] I regret the times I took even a few steps with you without taking your hand. I'm sorry for all the times I looked at you and I thought "My God, she's beautiful!" but didn't say it […] I love you and my deepest wish, the most permanent which accompanies me at all times, night and day, is that this is all over and that I have time enough to give you what I have not given you until today.
I love you, my bonsai.

Excerpt from a letter sent by Gerardo to Adriana on their thirteen wedding anniversary

YOU WILL NOT SEE A PICTURE OF ADRIANA AND GERARDO TAKEN IN PRISON

because the United States government, in a flagrant human rights violation, has repeatedly denied her a visa since he was arrested in 1998.

Logotype designed by Gerardo in his Lompoc prison. Today, this symbol, which stands for the struggle for the freedom of the Cuban Five, is known all over the world.

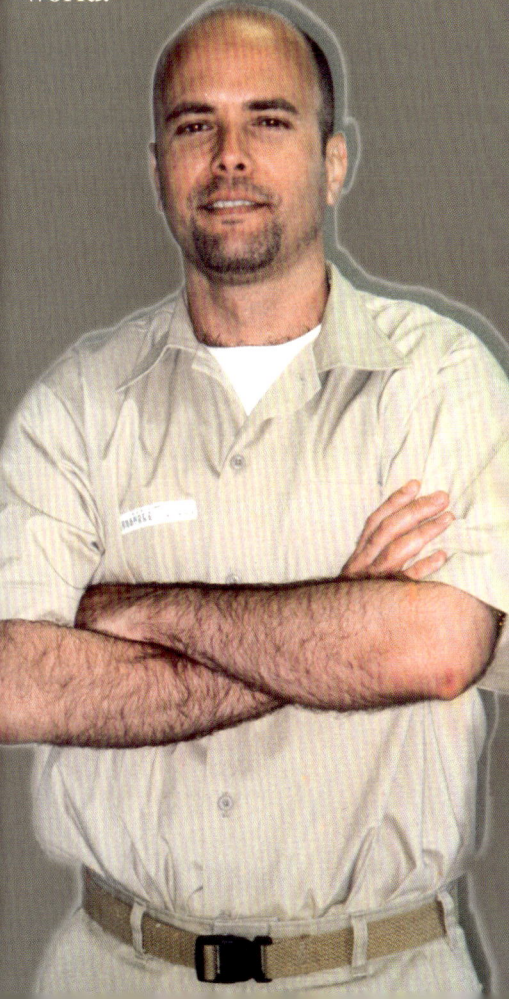

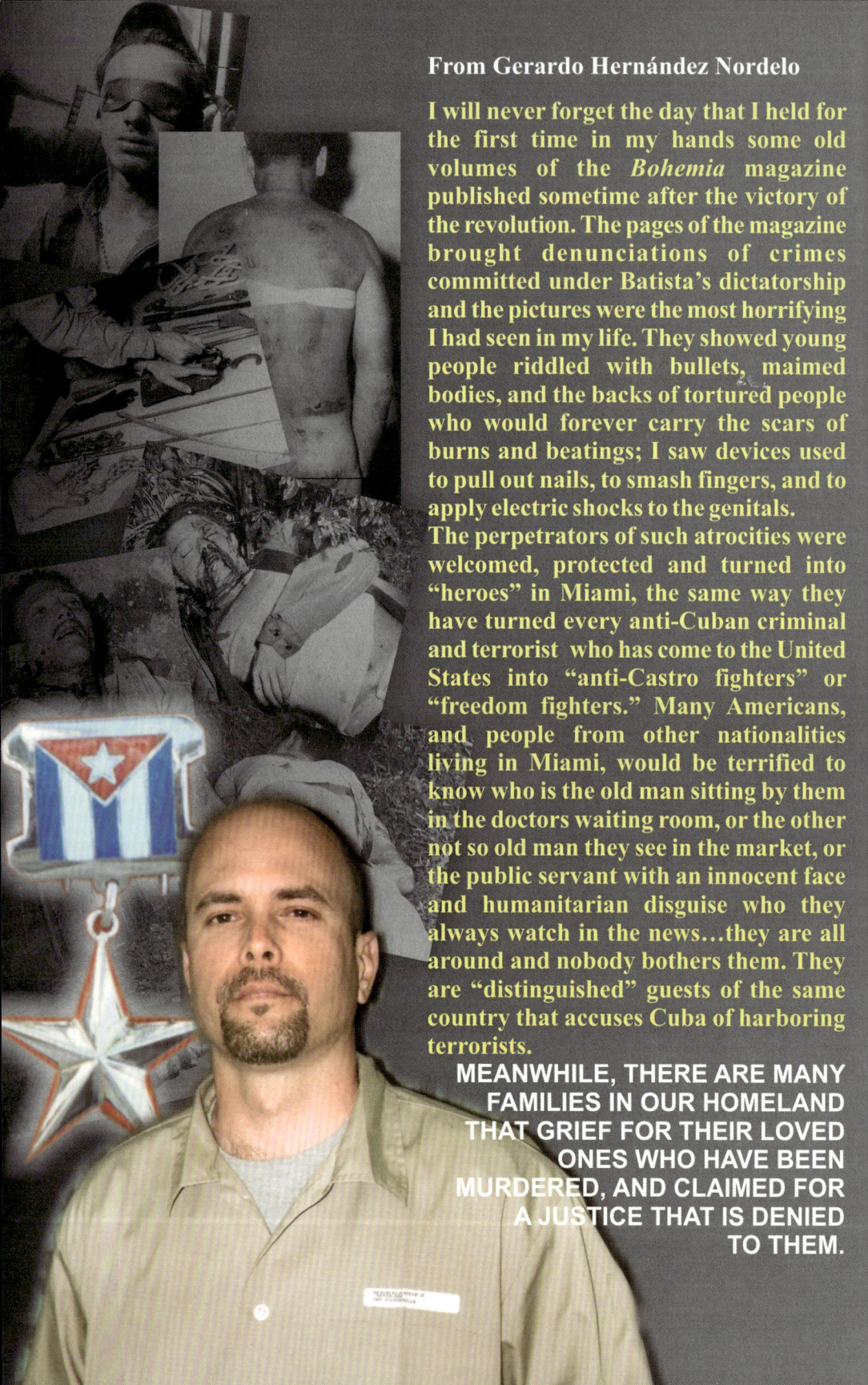

From Gerardo Hernández Nordelo

I will never forget the day that I held for the first time in my hands some old volumes of the *Bohemia* magazine published sometime after the victory of the revolution. The pages of the magazine brought denunciations of crimes committed under Batista's dictatorship and the pictures were the most horrifying I had seen in my life. They showed young people riddled with bullets, maimed bodies, and the backs of tortured people who would forever carry the scars of burns and beatings; I saw devices used to pull out nails, to smash fingers, and to apply electric shocks to the genitals.

The perpetrators of such atrocities were welcomed, protected and turned into "heroes" in Miami, the same way they have turned every anti-Cuban criminal and terrorist who has come to the United States into "anti-Castro fighters" or "freedom fighters." Many Americans, and people from other nationalities living in Miami, would be terrified to know who is the old man sitting by them in the doctors waiting room, or the other not so old man they see in the market, or the public servant with an innocent face and humanitarian disguise who they always watch in the news…they are all around and nobody bothers them. They are "distinguished" guests of the same country that accuses Cuba of harboring terrorists.

MEANWHILE, THERE ARE MANY FAMILIES IN OUR HOMELAND THAT GRIEF FOR THEIR LOVED ONES WHO HAVE BEEN MURDERED, AND CLAIMED FOR A JUSTICE THAT IS DENIED TO THEM.

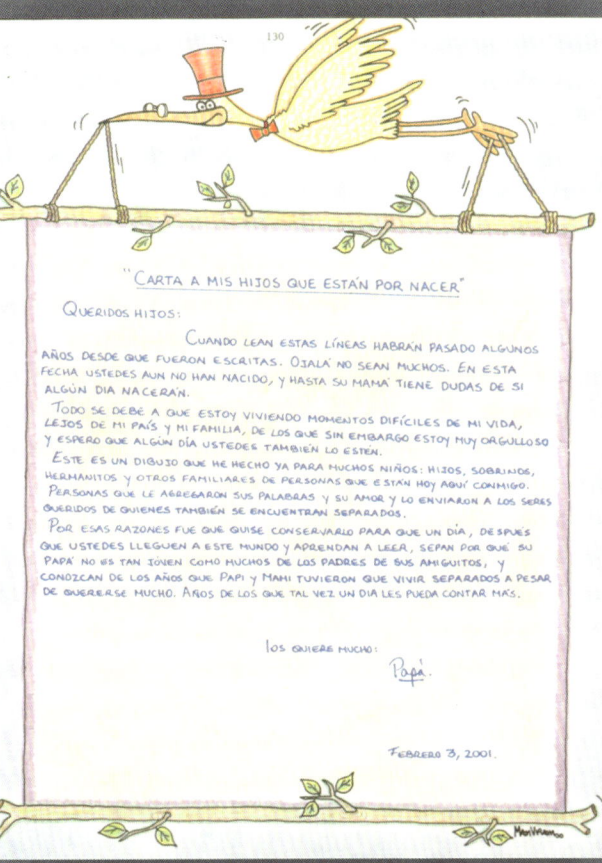

"Letter to my children who have not been born yet"

Dear children:

When you read these lines many years would have passed since they were written. I wish they are not too many. This moment you have not been born yet, and even your mother is uncertain that you'll be born one day.

This is because I'm experiencing difficult times in my life, far from my country and my family, of whom I am very proud, and I hope one day you too will be proud.

This drawing I made for many children: the sons and daughters, nieces and nephews, sisters and brothers and other relatives of people who are with me here today. These people have added their words and love and sent it to their loved ones from whom they too are separated.

It was for these reasons that I decided to keep it so that one day, after you come into this world and learn how to read, you can know why your dad is not as young as your friends' fathers and you may know of the years that Daddy and Mommy had to spend away from each other despite their big love, years about which I will perhaps one day tell you more.

I love you very much,

Dad

February 3, 2001

Unnecessarily punitive:
Amnesty International calls for temporary visas to be granted to two wives of the 'Cuban Five.'

Amnesty International is once again urging the US authorities to stringently review its decision to deny temporary visas to the wives of two Cuban nationals serving long federal prison sentences in the USA, and, in the absence of reasonable and conclusive evidence for continuing for them to be withheld, to grant them temporary visitation visas so that they may visit their husbands in the US.

Ref: AMR 51/01/06
Kevin Whitaker
Cuban Bureau
US State Department
Washington, DC 20520
USA

January 11, 2006
Dear Mr. Whitaker:

Amnesty International has written to the US government previously regarding Gerardo Hernández Nordelo, Ramón Labañino, Antonio Guerrero, Fernando Gonzáles and René Gonzáles (commonly known as the "Miami Five") who were sentenced to lengthy prison terms in the USA after being convicted of conspiracy to act as agents of the Cuban government and related charges. One of the issues on which we have raised concern is the US government's decision to deny René Gonzáles and Gerardo Hernández visits with their wives. Olga Salanueva, wife of René Gonzáles (sentenced to 15 years' imprisonment), has been refused entry to the USA since 2002…

Mrs. Adriana Pérez, wife of Gerardo Hernández (sentenced to life imprisonment), has not been permitted to visit her husband since his arrest in 1998. International standards emphasize the importance of prisoners maintaining regular contact with their families, including through visits. We are concerned that the long-term, permanent denial of visits from their immediate families has caused substantial hardship to René Gonzáles and Gerardo Hernández beyond the penalties imposed…
Such denial of family visits for convicted prisoners would represent a substantial hardship in any case. This is of even more urgent concern in the present cases given the serious questions which have been raised about the fairness of the convictions…

I look forward to receiving your response.

Yours sincerely,

Susan Lee
Program Director
Americas Regional Program

leonard weinglass
ian thompson

Some key questions about the Cuban Five

Civil rights attorney Leonard Weinglass represents Antonio Guerrero, one of the Cuban prisoners unjustly incarcerated in the U.S. for defending their homeland. As the legal team and supporters of the Five awaited the 11th Circuit Court of Appeals' decision on the case, lawyer Ian Thompson interviewed Weinglass about the Cuban Five and the importance of the case for the U.S. and Cuba.

Who are the Cuban Five? Why are they imprisoned in the United States?

The Cuban Five are five men who came to the United States in the early 1990s in response to the wave of violence directed at Cuba by mercenary groups from the Cuban exile community in southern Florida. Their names are Gerardo Hernández, Antonio Guerrero, Ramón Labañino, Fernando González and René González.

The Five were sent by the Cuban government unarmed and without any plan to inflict harm on the U.S. Their sole purpose was to monitor the network of terrorist groups that had been attacking Cuba since the triumph of the Revolution.

They came at a particular time in the history of the Cuban Revolution. Cuban's number one trading partner, the Soviet Union, had recently collapsed, and the economy of Cuba had gone into freefall. The Cuban government decided that one of the ways to restore economy health in Cuba was to engage in the tourist industry. The tourist industry was built up in 1992-93 and was an ongoing concern through 1994-95. In response, the mercenary wing of the Cuban exile community in South Florida decided to begin a violent terror campaign against the tourist industry as a way of undercutting the Cuban economy.

Bombs were placed in various hotels by anti-Cuban terrorists, in one instance killing an Italian tourist. A bomb was placed in the Havana airport. Bombs were placed in buses to and from the airport. The Cuban government protested these terrorist activities to the U.S., but to no avail. They protested to the United Nations, also without a response. As a result, beginning in the 1994-95 period, the Cuban Five came forward to protect their country.

The Five quickly succeeded in infiltrating the groups and reporting warnings to Cuba of the plans being developed to attack Cuba. In 1996-97, the U.S. government became aware of their presence in this country, and the FBI rounded them up in 1998. Three were charged with conspiracy to commit espionage; one was charged with conspiracy to commit murder.

A Miami jury convicted them on all counts after a seven-month trial. The trial of the Five was the longest trial in the history of the U.S. at the time. During the trial, the attorneys for the Five requested a change of venue from Miami to another city five times. The judge denied each request.

In December 2001, two of the Five were sentenced to life in prison, one to 19 years and one to 15 years. Gerardo Hernández received two life terms.

Why is it not possible for Cuban nationals like the Five to receive a fair trial in Miami? What role do anti-Cuban terrorists play?

Miami is the one city in the U.S. where the Five certainly could not receive a fair trial. There are approximately 650,000 Cubans who live there in exile. A group of them controls the local press and the media; they occupy the public offices, and they are the major business figures in the area. These individuals and institutions are highly influential, and they all have one thing in common: they take a hard line on Cuba. Miami is a different place than every other city in the U.S.

A portion of the exile community has engaged in terrorism against Cuba for decades. Violence against Cuba is heralded in small, but vocal, circles in Miami. For instance, in Miami, the terrorist Orlando Bosch walks the streets a free man. The U.S. Justice Department once labelled Bosch the most dangerous terrorist in the Western Hemisphere. He was responsible for bombing a Cuban passenger airline in mid-flight in 1976, killing all 73 passengers on board.

Hard-line exiles and their supporters play a large role in shaping public opinion and debate in Miami.

To try the Five in Miami was a clear violation of their right to have a trial free of outside influence that was prejudiced against them. The venue of the trial should have been moved out of Miami to another location.

Could you talk about how the charge of "conspiracy" is used generally, and how it was used specifically against the Five?

The Five were not charged with espionage. Rather, three of the Five —Gerardo, Antonio and Ramón— were charged with conspiracy to commit espionage. Conspiracy has always been the charge used by the prosecution in political cases.

A conspiracy is an agreement between people to commit a substantive crime. By using the charge of conspiracy, the government is relieved of the requirement that the underlying crime be proven. All the government has to prove to a jury is that there was an agreement to do the crime. The individuals charged with conspiracy are convicted even if the underlying crime was never committed.

In the case of the Five, the Miami jury was asked to find that there was an agreement to commit espionage. The government never had to prove that espionage actually happened. It could not have proven that espionage occurred. None of the Five sought or possessed any top secret information or U.S. national defense secrets. Yet, three of the Five were convicted of entering into an agreement to commit espionage. And that is what the government sought to convince a jury drawn from Miami: "Although we can't prove it, there certainly must have been an agreement to do it."

The sentence for the conspiracy charge is the same as if espionage were actually committed and proven. That is how three got life sentences.

The major charges in this case were all conspiracy related, the most serious being conspiracy to commit murder levied against Gerardo Hernández. The government charged Gerardo with conspiracy to commit murder based on the February 24, 1996, shoot down of two "Brothers to the Rescue" planes that illegally entered Cuban airspace.

What is the real reason that the U.S. has targeted the Five?

The U.S., in an effort to protect its own terrorist network, sought to stop these five men who had so successfully monitored the mercenary groups operating out of Florida.

But there is a broader context. There have been groups like the Five who have come to the U.S., just as the U.S. has gone to other countries, in an effort to infiltrate organizations that threaten the home country. To my knowledge, none of these groups have been prosecuted.

In this instance, however, we are dealing with Cuba. Cuba is handled differently that all other countries in the U.S. criminal justice system, in our immigration system, and in our exchanges with other countries.

There are certain U.S. policies and tactics reserved solely for dealing with the Cuban Revolution. Most recently, the U.S. rejected the visas of 61 Cuban scholars who applied to attend the Latin American Studies Association conference in Las Vegas. This case was handled in similar vein and should be seen as an extension of the overriding U.S. policy toward Cuba.

Ordinarily, if five people caught in the U.S. were working for another country, they would simply be returned to their home country. This is especially true if, like the Five, they were not armed and did not inflict injury or property damage. However, in this instance three of the Five are doing life and two are doing very long prison terms. That kind of hostile treatment is reserved solely for the Cuban Revolution.

You represent Antonio Guerrero, one of the Cuban Five. What is he as a person?

I spoke to Antonio just two days ago. We are constantly in touch with each other. Most often by letter, but occasionally we can speak by telephone. He is a remarkable person, a man of high principles and integrity, and obviously strong and courageous. He is also a poet with a poet's sentiments and feelings. His expression is marvellous and always very touching and direct.

Antonio went to prison in Florence, Colorado —one of the most difficult prisons in the United States— with the government hoping he would be treated roughly by other prisoners, especially those who are Cuban exiles. They hoped he would have a hard time because he was, in their view, a convicted spy, As it turns out, Antonio is beloved by the other prisoners. He is a teacher within the prison.

Over a year ago, when Antonio was removed from his class and subjected to very harsh treatment in solitary confinement, his students went on strike. I can see when I visit him that he is respected not only by other prisoners but by the guards as well.

Antonio's situation is similar to that which developed around Nelson Mandela during his long imprisonment. By virtue of the way Mandela conducted himself, he won other people over. They respected him, they felt very close and secure with him. It is the same way with Antonio.

It is a pleasure and a great honor for me to be part of his defense team.

You are one of the most highly regarded civil rights lawyers in the United States, having represented such noted figures on the left as Angela Davis, Abbie Hoffman, Mumia Abul-Jamal, the Chicago 8, the Los Angeles 8, and many more. Why did you get involved in the case of the Cuban Five?

The case is remarkable because it involves both an injustice abroad —U.S. policy toward Cuba— and an injustice at home —the way the Five were treated after their arrest and during their trial.

This is precisely the kind of case that I enjoy being a part of. It is political in nature and involves foreign policy as well as domestic issues. I feel very privileged to have been asked to work on this case.

On Friday, March 9, 2007, the Catholic Bishop of the Detroit's Archdioceses Thomas J. Gumbleton visited Fernando Gonzalez LLort at the Oxford penitentiary in Wisconsin. It was the first visit by a senior authority from the American clergy to one of the Five Cubans imprisoned in the United States since 1998.

Upon learning of the US Administration's injustice on the Five Cubans, Gumbleton, who was the founding chairman of Pax Christi in the United States, was interested in visiting one of the Fives to offer his support and solidarity.

The Bishop, one of the top leaders of the peace movement in America, has espoused many just causes and is presently a strong opponent of the Bush Administration's war in Iraq. On March 2005, Gumbleton, together with Noam Chomsky, Alice Walker, Nobel Peace Prize Rigoberta Menchu and others, signed a paid advertisement in The New York Times on the case of the Cuban Five.

The Bishop spoke with Fernando for several hours; they hit it off right away. According to Gumbleton, "Fernando and I have more things in common than I thought", and he added, "Fernando is in his prime; he is a sincere and receptive person and he is very much updated on world events including those related to the Catholic Church."

What most impressed the Bishop was that Fernando didn't speak only of his case or the Five's case but of the cause of the Cuban people fighting for its independence and sovereignty. Gumbleton could find in Fernando a great determination and devotion, a willingness to make the ultimate sacrifice if need be, including his own freedom for the well being of his homeland.

The Bishop has said that Fernando's morale is very high and that he looks physically strong and healthy. To Gumbleton, this points to his optimism not only about the victory of the Cuban Five but also on the victory of Cuba.

lisandro otero

The Five will be back

It was in 1959, when Batista's dictatorship plummeted, that the United States government started to promote actions to overthrow the nascent Cuban revolution. An anti-imperialist popular regime was more than it was willing to permit in its safe backyard of acquiescent sheep. Terrorism, sabotages, attacks with incendiary bombs, assassination attempts, chemical warfare, economic blockade, diplomatic isolation, political isolation and attempts at boycotting by the international economic community were organized with devastating efficacy.

Under Batista's tyranny numerous youth were found dead in the streets showing burns on their skin, the extraction of nails or the amputation of the tongue. These were signs of tortures suffered at the hands of cruel thugs like Esteban Ventura Novo, Conrado Carratalá or José María Salas Cañizares.

With the triumph of the Revolution on January 1959, all of that was left behind never to return. Then, thousands of schools were established, hundreds of hospitals, scores of universities and publishing houses, books, medications and sports stadiums. On the other hand, endemic diseases, illiteracy and extreme poverty were eradicated. Cuba is today a modest country where luxury items that abound in consumer societies can hardly be found but where there is a space with dignity and honor for everyone who wants to live with honesty and decency.

Successive US administrations would refuse to accept that a Latin American country had decided to live independently from its imperial edicts. They could not allow a strayed sheep to become a fighting bull. The moral example that such behavior set for the other docile and disciplined sheep was not welcomed by the almighty masters. As of this moment they started to hatch countless plans against Cuba, which had no choice but to resort to equally powerful friends that provided the means for its protection, at the same time it implemented strict rules that would allow it to survive.

One of the actions orchestrated to cause damage and devastation, and to force the country to go broke was a large invasion organized only to be defeated in Playa Girón. Other actions designed to bring sorrow to this country have included systematic accusations at the Human Rights Commission in Geneva aimed at discrediting the island and at having it confined to the dock. Actually, true human rights couldn't be further from this diplomatic exercise.

The United States is really trying to punish the island for its autonomous criteria, its independence, its emancipation from the imperial yoke and its distance from the flock of docile sheep that follow the bell rang by the imperial ringleader. Cuba is no longer a subjugated colony, a crushed or accepting province. Cuba today has its own voice and its own views emancipated from the traditional submission of the Latin American governments. Cuba has decided to act in accordance with the interests of the Cuban people and not the authoritarian ambitions of an expanding imperialism.

The true conflict has nothing to do with Cuba being a socialist country since the United States keeps intensive commercial and diplomatic relations with several socialist countries. The answer is simple: they want to remove the example of Cuba, to annihilate a model of breaking-off from the chain of vassalage, of getting rid of the infamous collar of serfdom carried by other Latin American countries.

Every state in the hemisphere must learn the lesson well: whoever tries to think with its own mind, to act differently and to decide by itself will stand to suffer the consequences of its rebelliousness and will be harassed by the packs of Castañeda-like hounds that unfortunately abound in our continent. Cuba has never accepted interference in its sovereignty. During the Missile Crisis, when the island was on the verge of becoming atomic dust, it did not accept the oversight mission headed by then UN Secretary U-Thant. Humiliating mediations were not accepted.

What has the Cuban Revolution done to elicit such biased challenge? It has given the land to the farmers who tilt it and recuperated the national wealth for the benefit of its people. The overwhelming majority of those who were house tenants, today own their houses. Illiteracy was eradicated and free education provided to every Cuban child. Today, Cuba ranks first in the world in the number of teachers per capita and of children in a classroom. The children with disabilities have special schools to attend to. University students have received economic assistance at a time when university campuses have proliferated all over the country. Infant mortality rate has been reduced to six per one thousand live births, the lowest in the continent, while life expectancy has been raised by fifteen years. The implementation of massive vaccination campaigns has eradicated formerly endemic diseases. Cuba is the country in the world with the highest number of physicians per capita, and the entire healthcare system is free of charge for all citizens. Research centers have been established that produce vaccines and preventive solutions against many diseases.

The Cuban film industry is widely respected and admired, the same as its visual arts. A powerful literary movement has emerged in the last decades; publishing houses have grown and book production with them. Theaters, museums, art galleries, concert halls and conservatories keep expanding their creative influence. The successes of the Cuban athletes prove the efficiency of a network of sport facilities and of a system of promotion of physical development.

There is no torture in Cuba —none of its accusers has been able to prove it beyond doubt— and extrajudicial executions are unknown here. Unlike the rest of Latin America, the category of "disappeared" does not exist in Cuba. Is that what its enemies want to eliminate? Shall Cuba give in before a messianic and lunatic ruler like Bush? Shall Cuba succumb to the rabid onslaught of its antagonists mobilized from Washington? Of course, not. Cuba will resist and Cuba will survive!

But, in order to organize its defense Cuba needed to know its enemy's plans, to anticipate its aggressive intentions; and it became necessary to infiltrate the ranks of its adversaries with those who could forewarn of the attacks that would come. In June 1998, the Cuban government passed on to officers of US law enforcement agencies a memorandum with evidence of the terrorist attempts being hatched against Cuba. That information indicated that various organizations there were designing a crisis that would be conducive to an attack or invasion by the United States army. The purpose of such revelation was to have the FBI put an end to the activities of the anti-Cuban extremists, but far from acting against the terrorists, the FBI focused on finding out where the information came from. They then discovered that five young men, René González, Antonio Guerrero, Fernando González, Gerardo Hernández and Ramón Labañino, had been the ones to alert on the criminal intentions of the sworn fanatics among the Miami exiles. The five men were then arrested and accused of espionage.

It was outrageous that such a conspiracy was orchestrated against a small country while a group of agents from large transnational corporations, entrenched in the White House, were on the eve of unleashing the most unjust, illegal and unjustifiable predatory operation on the Middle East oil. A new Nuremberg Tribunal would be required to judge Bush, Cheney, Rumsfeld and Condolezza instead of little helpless Cuba. A war tribunal should be established to pass judgment on the genocide committed against the Iraqi people, the destruction of Humanity's Cultural Heritage in Baghdad, and many other acts of barbarism and savagery perpetrated by the US troops. Why so much rigor towards the little ones and so much leniency towards the powerful?

During the trial of The Five, the accusers could never prove that the defendants had even tried to obtain secrets related to the national security of the United States, or that they ever tried to plot against the stability of the American society. Their sole interest was finding out about terrorist actions and reporting them to Cuba; that would be all. Over seventy witnesses testified at the trial. The trial record spread into 119 volumes of transcriptions, in addition to 15 other volumes of statements and testimonies.

Various senior US military men stated that the use of the open sources of information by The Five could not be construed as an act of espionage. Not one of The Five was found to be in possession of one page of classified information of the US government. However, the ardent, feverish and frenzied atmosphere created by the old exiles succeeded in obtaining from a Jury three life sentences and two 19 and 15 years sentences, respectively. The Five were isolated in federal prisons and subjected to harsh prison conditions, while preventing the visits of relatives.

Their sentences were appealed in May 2003 at an Atlanta Court, since Miami was not the proper place for an unbiased evaluation of the case given the exacerbated hatred of one sector of the Cuban community living there. On August 2005 the Atlanta Court of Appeals ruled in favor of revoking the sentences and holding a new trial. Meanwhile, the obvious bias of the Miami court, the stubborn harassment of the extremist Cuban exiles and the unquestionable injustice gave rise to a wave of world solidarity with the prisoners.

There are over two hundred committees for the freedom of The Five in seventy-five countries. Fifteen hundred personalities from all over the world, six Nobel Laureates among them, have signed a document demanding the end of the arbitrary situation and claiming for the release of the five prisoners. The world scandal provoked by this outrage, stirred up by the hatred of the intransigent Cubans in Miami, has proven the obvious violation of the law in the infamy conceived against the five who only tried to defend their country.

In Cuba we are confident that The Five will be back home someday. We are all convinced that the Bush regime will not be able to trample on the law indefinitely.

At some point in history, the American people will become aware of the abyss where the government of the big oil companies has taken them, and an Administration will come that will act sensibly. Then justice will advance and The Five, who are unjustly kidnapped, will finally be released.

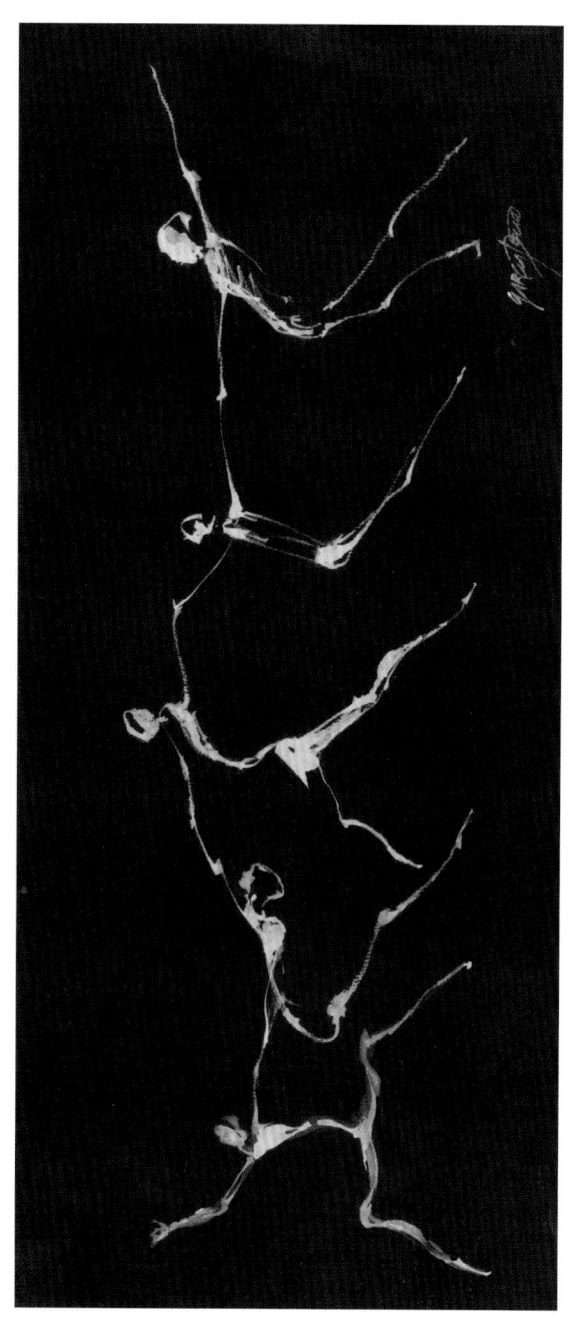

Dance of the Innocent   Ernesto García Peña

# ricardo alarcón de quesada

Epilogue

Miami was discovered at the end of the 20th century. It was not the work of daring navigators but of hundreds of journalists and cameramen. Thanks to modern technology, for several months a state of barbarism broke into homes all over the world.

    Day and night all you could see on every TV screen was the scum of the earth, the Mafiosi testing the Law, the Federal Government and the Courts refusing to return to his father a six-year-old boy who had just lost his mother and become the victim of the most publicized kidnapping and child mistreatment in history. Millions could watch and listen to the Mayor and the Police Commissioner, legislators and politicians, business people, priests and local newsmen all-together backing the kidnappers. It was a disgusting show and most Americans were outraged. There was relief all over the planet when, ultimately, a commando force especially sent from Washington assaulted the place, disarmed the bandits and rescued Elián González.

    But nobody knew that, simultaneously, five young Cubans were also kidnapped in Miami. For long months they had been kept incommunicado; they were being punished because they had put their lives on the line to fight against *that* terrorist mob. Separated from the rest of the world, isolated in punishment cells for seventeen months, unable to even defend themselves, they became the targets of a grotesque and abhorrent judicial farce. Their defense lawyers uselessly tried to move the trial to another city; the Prosecution flatly refused. The Five had to be punished in Miami, a decency-offending city most unfairly described as "cosmopolitan and diverse."

The selection of the Jury would be an unusually revealing spectacle. Tens of people summoned to do jury duty spoke openly of their prejudices against Cuba and against the five defendants and confessed their impossibility to pass an unbiased judgment but also the fear to lose their lives or put their relatives' in jeopardy if they dared to dissent from what the city mobsters were demanding.

It was not until August 2005 that the three judges tasked by the Atlanta Court of Appeals to review the case decided to annul it, the reason being that holding the trial in Miami was considered by these worthy magistrates a denial of justice that impinged on the basic principles enshrined in the Constitution of the United States. They unanimously set forth a solid and convincing 93-page text, which serves today as a case study in various Law Schools of that country's universities.

But, a surprise awaited the experts a year later when, following a request from the US Attorney General, a full panel of judges annulled the document that three of its members had approved.

Holding that trial in Miami obviously pointed to a fraudulent behavior on the part of the Attorney's Office. This sufficed to declare the entire procedure inconsistent, null and without merit, and to immediately release the Five. There were many other violations and every one of them would have justified the dismissal of the forged accusations and the end of the shameful process.

The detention of the Five and keeping them unjustifiably in solitary confinement for seventeen months in clear violation of the penitentiary's rules; their extreme difficulty to communicate with the outside world, including their own defense lawyers; the refusal to give them access to the alleged evidence supporting the accusations, something being challenged by the defense still today, May 2007; the inflammatory speeches made by the Prosecution, which combined with the systematic campaign of the local press aimed at sawing confusion and scaring the members of the Jury; the direct pressures of members of the Miami Mafia, even inside the Court building, which led the Judge to protest it more than once; any of these events would have led to the annulment of the charges, the dismissal of the case and the release of the defendants, of course, in a US Court of Law where a normal trial is held.

These were the events weighed up by the United Nations Working Group on Arbitrary Detentions when it determined, two years ago, that the trial against the Five was arbitrary and contrary to International Law, and demanded from the US Administration that, in compliance with its obligations, put an end to this situation.

Now, when our compatriots have spent almost nine years unfairly and cruelly imprisoned, the Court of Appeals has yet to complete its case revision.

We are still waiting for that Court to fully dismiss the second charge –that is, conspiracy to commit espionage— for which Gerardo, Ramón and Antonio are serving life sentences. This charge is completely baseless since they were not found to possess any secret. Even the Pentagon stated in an official declaration that nothing in this case had affected the national security of the United States while before the Miami Court, and various American senior officers, Generals and Admirals included, testified under oath that they had seen no hint of espionage or the intent to do anything of the sort.

We keep waiting for the Court to throw away the infamous third charge of conspiracy to commit first degree murder, for which Gerardo was given a second life sentence, since in an unprecedented action the government has admitted before that same Atlanta Court that it was unable to prove the stupid accusation and requested its dismissal.

Everything I have written here can be corroborated by reading the Miami Federal Court minutes, available in the Internet under the heading "*United States versus Gerardo Hernandez et al*". There, too, the key can be found to the disciplined, standard silence imposed by the most important "media." The Five were arrested, indicted and cruelly punished for infiltrating the terrorist groups operating with impunity against Cuba. They were trying to discover these groups' criminal plans and save lives. This fact was repeatedly recognized by the Prosecution, that is, by the United States administration, which acted with such indecency because it knew it could count on the obedience of the media bent on hiding the truth.

The present book, the work of some of the best Cuban artists and writers, comes as a beautiful contribution to the battle we shall continue waging to make the truth prevail.

Asked by the San Luis Publishing House to write this epilogue I've done it with a sense of duty and the certainty that the true epilogue of this story will be written by many when Gerardo, Ramón, Antonio, Fernando and René are back home; when we can embrace them as free men, here in their homeland for which they have sacrificed their lives, so that they can receive from their people, as the Beatles put it in their last song, "the love you take is equal to the love you make."

THE SENTENCES

◄ ANTONIO:
SENTENCED TO ONE LIFE SENTENCE PLUS 10 YEARDS, FOR FIGHTING TERRORISM

FERNANDO: ►
SENTENCED TO 19 YEARS IN PRISON, FOR FIGHTING TERRORISM

RAMÓN: ►
SENTENCED TO ONE LIFE SENTENCE PLUS 18 YEARS, FOR FIGHTING TERRORISM

◄ RENÉ:
SENTENCED TO FIFTEEN YEARS IN PRISON FOR FIGHTING TERRORISM

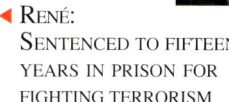

GERARDO: ►
SENTENCED TO TWO LIFE SENTENCES PLUS 15 YEARS, FIGHTING TERRORISM

THE AUTHORS

Roberto Fernández Retamar (Havana, 1930). He studied in the University of Havana, where he is a Professor Emeritus, and in universities in Paris and London. He has dictated courses and lectured in universities of Latin America, Europe and Japan, some of which have presented him with Honorary Doctorate Degrees. He is president of Casa de las Americas since 1986. He has an extensive bibliography, recognized the world over, which includes among his most acclaimed tittles *Elegia como un himno*, 1950; *La poesia contemporanea en Cuba, 1927-1953,* 1954; and, *Concierto para la mano izquierda*, 2001. In 1989, he was accorded the National Literature Award.

Cintio Vitier (Key West, La Florida, 1921). Awarded the 1988 National Literature Prize, Cintio Vitier was one of the members of the *Grupo Orígenes* and the homonymous magazine. His work includes poetry, essay, narration and translation. He is a scholar specialized in the work of José Martí and one of the most outstanding poets and essayists of Cuba. Some works outstand in his fruitful life, such as *Lo cubano en la poesía*, 1958; *Ese sol del mundo moral* and *Para una historia de la etnicidad cubana*, 1975; Poesía escogida and other relevant texts.

Adagio Benítez (Santiago de Cuba, 1924). A painter, a poet and professor, Benitez goes way back in the history of visual arts in Cuba. He is an experienced professor and curator of Cuban arts exhibits. He received the 2002 National Visual Arts Award and the 2003 National Artistic Education Award. His works are displayed with the Collection of Cuban Art in the National Museum of Fine Arts as well as in other public and private collections.

Frank Fernández (Mayarí, 1944). A pianist and a professor, a producer and composer, Frank Fernández has performed as a solo pianist with over one hundred orchestras from Europe, Asia and Latin America. At the Prague Spring Festival he was chosen to play the Tchaikovski *Concierto No.1* in the Smetana auditorium where said work was first presented by its author. His catalogue includes over six hundred and fifty works for various formats. He has been awarded numerous prizes and citations such as a Prize to the best original sound track for films, radio and TV as well as four Grand Prix for arrangements at the Adolfo Guzman and Benny Moré Contests. He has been described as a Steinway Artist.

Daniel Chavarría (1933). Narrator, professor of Latin and Greek languages, translator, and script writer for films and TV, Chavarría is a Uruguayan living in Cuba since 1969. The author of many important novels, Chavarría has been deservedly awarded numerous national and international awards, among them: *Joy*, 1978 MININT Prize; *Allá ellos*, 1992 Dashiell Hammett Prize; *El ojo de cibeles*, 1993 Planeta-Joaquin Mortiz Prize; *Adios muchachos*, New York Edgar Allan Poe 2002 Prize; and, *Viudas de sangre*, Alejo Carpentier 2002 Prize.

Enrique Ávila González (Holguín, 1952). A graduate from the Provincial School of Visual Arts, Avila is a painter, sculptor and set designer. He has showed his works in numerous individual and collective exhibits. His most universally recognized work is his Che Guevara sculpture in relief permanently displayed at the Revolution Square.

Lázaro Silvestre García (Cienfuegos, 1947). A guitar player, composer and writer, Silvestre García is one of the founders of the Nueva Trova musical movement in Cuba. He has performed in many countries of Latin America, Europe and Africa. He has composed music for films and plays. He has been awarded the Adolfo Guzmán Cuban Music Prize, the Cucalambé Prize and the May 17 Literary Prize.

Marilyn Bobes (Havana, 1955). A poet, a narrator and editor, Marilyn Bobes has lectured in various American and European universities. Some of her outstanding works include *Alguien tiene que llorar*, which was awarded the Casa de las Américas 1995 Short Story Prize. She also received the Casa de las Américas 2005 Award for her novel *Fiebre de Invierno*. Her poems, reports and short stories have been translated to various languages and included in several anthologies.

Eduardo M. Abela (Havana, 1963). A graduate from the San Alejandro School of Fine Arts, Abela has taken part in numerous individual exhibits in Cuba and overseas. He was awarded the First Prize at the 1999 Salón Nacional de Humorismo and the Special Award and Prize from the Centro de Desarrollo de las Artes Visuales, during the DDT 2000 Segunda Bienal Internacional.

Robertico Carcassés (Havana, 1972). A graduate of the National School of Arts, Robertico Carcassés is a pianist, a composer and arranger. He is the leading figure in the creative space known as *Interactivo* which brings together the vanguard of Cuban and international music. He has been awarded the prize for Opera Prima, for Fusion Music, the DVD Jazz Cuba Today Prize and the Cubadisco 2006 Grand Prix.

Pablo Armando Fernández (Central Delicias, 1930). A poet, an essayist and novelist, Pablo Armando is also a playwright and a translator of English poetry. His books of poems include *Toda la poesía*, 1961; *Himnos*, 1962; *Libro de los héroes*, 1964; and, *Campo de amor y batalla*, 1984. Some of his most remarkable novels are *Los niños se despiden*, 1968; *El vientre del pez*, 1989; and, *Otro golpe de dados*, 1993. Pablo Armando's works have been translated to various European and Asian languages and compiled in numerous anthologies. He was awarded the 1996 Literature Prize.

Pucho López (Placetas, 1956). He has taken part in jazz festivals in Europe, Asia and the Americas. Pucho's work with a jazz-fusion troupe made him the recipient of the 1979 UNEAC Award. He has received, among others, the Danzon Special Prize on the 100th anniversary of this music genre. He was awarded the 1983 Radio Critique Prize.

Sándor González (Havana, 1977). A graduate from the San Alejandro School of Fine Arts in the year 2000, Sándor González's works can be found in many private and public collections in Argentina, Brazil, Denmark, Spain, the United States, Finland, France, England and other countries. He is one of the painters of the collective work *El Arca de la Libertad* displayed at the National Museum of Fine Arts of Cuba.

Ever Fonseca (Manzanillo, 1938). A painter, a sculptor and ceramist, Ever Fonseca, graduated from the National School of Visual Arts in Havana. For over twenty years he was a professor in three levels of artistic education. His work has been in display with a Permanent Collection at the National Museum of Fine Arts since 1970. His works can be found in the Americas and in the United Nations Cultural Heritage Collection.

Mylene Fernández Pintado (Pinar del Río, 1963). She received the 1998 David Award for her work *Anhedonia*. Her novel *Plegarias atendidas* was awarded the 2002 Italo Calvino Prize. Her stories have been translated into various languages and included in anthologies.

Polo Montañez (Sierra del Rosario, 1955 –Havana, 2002). Born in the countryside, Polo Montañéz had an innate musical gift, which showed in popular singing functions, as a percussionist and singer. He was a self-taught composer of more than one hundred sones, guarachas, ballads and other genres. He received the Golden Record Award for his *Guajiro natural* and the Platinum Record Award in Colombia 2001 for his *Guitarra mía*. He performed in Latin America and Europe. He was nicknamed Guajiro natural for the spontaneity of his interpretations.

Francisco López Sacha (Manzanillo, 1950). A narrator, an essayist and art professor, López Sacha is a graduate in Arts and a drama expert. He published his novel *El cumpleaños del fuego* in 1986 and 1990 and the short story books *La división de las aguas*, 1987; *Descubrimiento del azul*, 1987; and, *Análisis de la ternura*, 1988. He has compiled and authored the prologue of such anthologies as *Fábula de ángeles*, 1994, and *La isla contada*, 1996, both of them a great success with the critics and the public. *Pastel flameante*, 2006, brings together almost two decades of his work as a critic of literature, drama and other cultural subjects.

Manuel Comas (Havana, 1963). A graduate of the Higher School of Arts in 1987, Comas' work has been displayed in individual exhibits and can be found in private collections in Cuba, the United States, Spain, Portugal and France, and other countries.

Edel Morales (Cabaiguán, 1961). He was awarded the 1984 Pinos Nuevos Prize for his book of poems *Viendo los autos pasar hacia occidente*. He has published *Escritura visible*, 1999, and he authored the prologue of the catalogue of young Cuban poets *Cuerpo, sobre cuerpo, sobre cuerpo*, 2000 and *La estrella de Cuba (Inventory of an expedition)*, 2004. His book of poems *Lejos de la corriente* exposes the reader to the best of his poetry.

Eduardo Heras León (Havana, 1940). A narrator and professor, a journalist and editor, and a literary critic, Heras León received the 2001 National Award for Edition. He has lectured on narration techniques and Cuban literature in Canada, the United States, Latin America and Europe. Some of his most reknown books are *La Guerra tuvo seis nombres*, awarded the 1968 David Prize; *Los pasos en la hierba*, a Casa de las Ameritas 1970 honorable mention; *Acero*, 1977 and *Cuestión de principios*, 1986. At the moment he chairs the Onelio Jorge Cardoso Center for Literary Training.

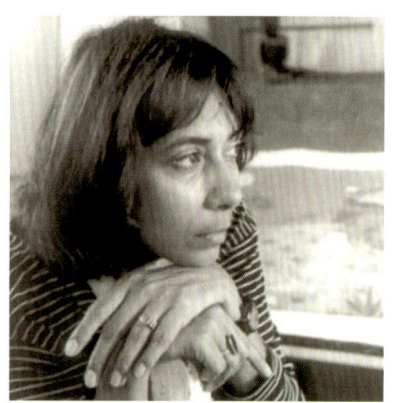

Alicia Leal (Sancti Spiritus, 1957). A graduate from the San Alejandro School of Fine Arts in 1980, Alicia Leal's works can be found in various private and permanent collections in the United States, Mexico, Jamaica, Spain, France, Germany, England, Japan and other countries. She received the Third National Award at the Salón Paisaje '90 and the Third Prize of the Faconnable French Firm in 1997.

Alejandro Leyva (Havana, 1970). A graduate painter from the National School of Arts, Leyva's works can be found in private collections in the United States, Mexico, Spain, Holland, Panama and other countries. He has been presented, among others, with the 1997 Abstract Painting Award and the UNEAC 2001 Drawing Award.

Flora Fong (Camaguey, 1949). A graduate from the Higher School of Arts, Flora Fong was a professor at the San Alejandro School of Fine Arts from 1970 through 1989. In 1985 she was awarded the International Visual Arts Prize in Havana, Cuba. She is one of the best known artists of her generation. Her works are featured in private collections and museums of Europe, Asia and the Americas.

Alberto Guerra (Havana, 1963). A narrator and professor, Guerra has published *Disparos en el aula*, 1992; *Aporias de la Feria,* 1994; and, *Blasfemias del escriba*, 2000. He has been awarded several prizes for his works of fiction. Some of his short stories have been translated into various languages and can be found in major anthologies. Some of these stories have been adapted for TV.

Juan Moreira (Havana, 1938). A graduate from the San Alejandro School of Fine Arts in 1963, Moreira's work is displayed in permanent collections of museums in Europe and the Americas, the United Nations venue in Geneva, and in the private collections of President James Carter and His Majesty Juan Carlos de Borbon.

Ernesto García Peña (Matanzas, 1949). A graduate from the Higher School of Art in 1987, García Peña was a professor of drawing, engraving and painting at the National School of Art in the 1970s and 1980s. His work can be found in the most important museums of the Americas and Europe, as well as in numerous private collections.

Miguel Mejides (Camaguey, 1950). He is a narrator who has published many books, including *Tiempo de hombres*, 1977; *El jardín de las flores silvestres*, awarded the 1983 UNEAC Prize; *Rumba Palace*, 1995; and the novels *Perversiones en el Prado*, 1999; and, *Amor con cabeza extrana*, 2006. He won the 1995 Juan Rulfo Award from Radio Francia Interncional.

Nelson Domínguez (Baire, 1947). A graduate from the National School of Arts in 1970, Domínguez has been a professor in that same school and the head of the Department of Painting in the Higher School of Arts where he has also been a member of the Department of Engraving. His extensive and rich work is featured in public collections in the Americas, Europe and Asia and in private collections like the Her Majesty's the Queen of Holland, Steven Spielberg's, Robert Redford's and Liv Ullmann's, among others.

Rafael Zarza (Havana, 1944). A graduate from the San Alejandro School of Fine Arts in 1965, Zarza is also a reknown lithography specialist. He was awarded the Casa de las Américas 1968 Portinari Lithography Prize. His extensive work is displayed in public institutions in Europe and the Americas, and in private collections in numerous countries.

Lisandro Otero (Havana, 1932). A novelist, a diplomat and journalist, Lisandro Otero was awarded the 2002 National Literature Prize. He is the President of the Cuban Academy of Language and a corresponding member of the Royal Spanish Academy of Language, and of the North American Academy of Spanish Language. His books, translated into fourteen languages, include novels, essays, testimonies and press reports. *La situación, Temporada de ángeles* and *Arbol de la vida* are some of his best known novels.

Jesús Orta Ruiz, *Indio Naborí* (Havana, 1922-2006). A poet and journalist, a literary researcher and folklore specialist, the Indio Naborí was awarded the 1995 National Literature Prize. Some of his texts have been translated into various languages and published in major anthologies in Cuba and overseas.

César López (Santiago de Cuba, 1933). Graduated as a medical doctor from the University of Salamanca in Spain, with previous studies in universities in Havana and Madrid, Cesar López has been a diplomat, a professor and translator. He is a full member of the Cuban Academy of Language and a corresponding member of the Royal Spanish Academy of Language. He was accorded the 1999 National Literature Award. His best known books of poems include *Silencio en voz de muerte, Primer libro de la ciudad, Segundo libro de la ciudad, Tercer libro de la ciudad, Paisaje, Panorama* and the book of stories *Circulando el cuadrado.*

Marta Rojas (Santiago de Cuba, 1931). A narrator, a journalist and war correspondent in Viet Nam, Marta Rojas has authored a unique testimony: *El juicio del Moncada.* She has received the Casa de las Américas 1978 Testimony Awarqqd for her work *El que debe vivir:* her book *La cueva del muerto,* 1983, was made into a film. She also wrote **El columpio del rey Spencer,** 1992; *Santa Lujuria,* 1998; *El haren de Oviedo,* 2002 and the novel Inglesa por un año, for which she was awarded the Alejo Carpentier 2006 Prize.

Alexis Leyva Machado, *Kcho* (Nueva Gerona, 1970).Graduated from the National School of Arts in 1990, Kcho's work has won a great number of prizes and citations. Some of the main collections showing his works are in the National Museum of Fine Arts and the University of Informatics Sciences; the Museum of Modern Art (MOMA) in New York; Peter Norton's private collection; the International Center of Contemporary Art in Montreal; the Reina Sofia Art Center at the National Museum in Madrid; and, the Pilar i Joan Miro Foundation in Mallorca, Spain.

Silvio Rodríguez, (San Antonio de los Baños, 1946). As a poet and composer, and a founding member of the *Nueva Trova Musical Movement* and the *Grupo de experimentación Sonora del ICAIC*, Silvio Rodríguez has been the auntor of over eight hundred works. As from 1997, he is a UNESCO Peace Artist. In 2007, he was presented with an Honorary Doctorate Degree at the University of San Marcos, Lima, Perú.

Ernesto Rancaño (Havana, 1968). A graduate of the San Alejandro School of Fine Arts, Rancaño was awarded the First Prize in the Posters Contest convened and sponsored by the CETSS in Havana. His works are featured in permanent collections in Panama, Mexico, Jamaica and Spain. He has also taken part in numerous collective exhibitions and art performing atmosphere.

Miguel Barnet (Havana, 1940). A writer, an ethnologist and poet, Miguel Barnet published in 1966 the widely acclaimed novel *Biografía de un Cimarrón*, considered a classic of Cuban literature. He has also published various books of poems such as *Mapa del tiempo, Viendo mi vida pasar*, and *Con pies de gato*. Several of his novels have been identified as testimonies; such is the case of *Canción de Rachel, Gallego, La vida real* and *Oficio de ángel*. He was awarded the 1994 National Literature Prize.

Nancy Morejón (Havana, 1944). A poet, an essayist and translator, Nancy Morejón has published over thirty-five books, among them *Richard trajo su flauta y otros argumentos*, 1967; and Awards for Critiques, *Piedra Pulida*, 1986; *La Quinta de los Molinos*, 2000; and *Cuerda Veloz*, 2002. She was presented with the National Literature Award, 2001.

Esteban A. Leyva (Havana, 1957). A graduate from the Higher Institute of Arts, Esteban Leyva has been for over a decade a professor and head of the department of Painting and Composition in the National School of Arts. His catalogue shows a remarkable number of individual and collective exhibits. His work is also treasured in private collections in the Americas, Europe and Australia. He received the 1986 National Painting Award.

Alejandro Valdés (Havana, 1962). A self-trained guitarist, Alejandro Valdes became known in 1978 with various music groups and accompanying great Cuban popular singers. He is also an outstanding solo player who has lately associated with jazz and classic music players.

Laidi Fernández de Juan (Havana, 1961). A graduated medical doctor since 1985, her first book *Dolly y otros cuentos africanos* received a prize during the first edition of Pinos Nuevos in 1994. Clemencia bajo el sol was awarded the 1996 Cecilia Valdés Grand Prix. *Oh Vida* received the 1999 Luis Felipe Rodríguez Cuentos de la UNEAC Prize. Her third book of short stories, *La hija de Darío*, was awarded the 2005 Alejo Carpentier National Prize. Her works can be found in numerous Cuban and foreign anthologies.

Javier Guerra Fernández (Havana, 1969). A graduate from the National School of Arts, Guerra Fernández has displayed his works in numerous individual and collective exhibits and received awards in various contests. His works have been displayed in galleries of Spain, the Dominican Republic and the United States.

José María Vitier (Havana, 1954). A pianist and composer, José Maria Vitier has composed music for films, TV, plays, ballet and dancing in addition to Chamber music, symphonies, religious music and music for children. One of his best known pieces is Misa cubana, which has been played in over twenty countries, and a selection of which was performed during the Mass said by Pope John Paul II in Havana, in 1998. He has been awarded numerous international and national prizes such as the 1989 Ocella Award, at the Venice Film Festival; the 1992 and 1999 Coral Awards at the International Film Festival of Havana; the Goya Prize in Spain and the Ariel Prize in Mexico.

Eduardo R. Salazar, *Choco* (Santiago de Cuba, 1949). Graduated from the National School of Arts, Choco's works are featured in collections in Mexico, the Miró Foundation in Palma de Mallorca, the Museum of the University of Tama an Kochi, Japan, and at the National Museum of Fine Arts in Cuba. He has received numerous national and international awards, including the UNEAC First Drawing Prize, the First Prize for Small Format Engraving in Orense, Spain, and the Triennial Grand Prix of Engraving from Kochi, Japan.

José Omar Torres (Matanzas, 1953). A painter and engraver, Torres has taken part in about one-hundred national and international exhibits. His works are displayed at the Gabinete de Estampa in the National Museum of Fine Arts in Cuba, the Schrainer Museum of Cologne, the Brandywine Workshop of Philadelphia and the Lehigh University Art Galleries Collection in the United States.

Ernán López-Nussa (Havana, 1958). A pianist and composer, the works of López-Nussa are already a part of Cuba's, the America's and the world's contemporary musical repertoire. He has been acclaimed as a virtuoso at the Ronnie Scott's of London, the Museum of Art in Los Angeles, the Municipal Theater of Rio de Janeiro, the Teresa Carreño Theater of Caracas, the Trastienda theater in Buenos Aires and the Fujiyama Jazz Festival in Japan.

Sergio Vitier (Havana, 1948). A guitar player and composer, Sergio Vitier is one of the most valuable and gifted artists of Cuban culture. He has authored over fifty sound tracks for films and TV. Another important area of work relates with theater, dancing and ballet. He has also worked with electro acoustic music, choirs, vaudeville theater and particularly symphonies and Chamber music thanks to his master knowledge of composition, arrangement and orchestration as well as his deep acquaintance with Cuba's popular musical traditions. He has an extensive list of records. Vitier has played his music in countless theaters all over the world.

Dr. Leonard I. Weinglass (United States, 1933). Weinglass has worked in cases marking American political history of social struggles in the last thirty years, such as, the Chicago Seven; the Pentagon Papers; Jane Fonda's lawsuit against Richard Nixon; the case of African American activist Angela Davis; and others. He is a member of the team of defense lawyers acting for the Cuban Five imprisoned in the United States for fighting terrorism.

Roberto Fabelo (Camaguey, 1950). Graduated from the National School of Arts in 1976 and the Higher School of Arts in 1981, Fabelo has displayed his works in both individual and collective exhibitions. The numerous awards he has received include a First Prize at the 10th International Drawing Biennial in Great Britain in 1993. Later, in 1996, he was awarded the First Prize at the 1st Ibero-American Watercolor Biennial in Viña del Mar, Chile. His self-portrait was chosen for the Permanent Collection of the Degli Uffizi gallery in Florence, Italy. He was awarded the National Visual Arts 2004 Prize.

Ricardo Alarcón de Quesada (Havana, 1937). A Doctor in Philosophy and Arts, and Full Professor in the University of Havana, Alarcón de Quesada was Cuban Permanent Ambassador to the United Nations for thirteen years and later a Minister of Foreign Affairs. In 1993 he was elected Speaker of the National Assembly of People's Power where he still holds that position. He is a member of the Cuban Communist Party's Political Bureau and a key player in United States-Cuba relations. Alarcón, a deeply cultured and outstanding politician with an incisive mind, holds a special place in the realm of Cuban intelligentsia today.

INDEX

Prologue ROBERTO FERNÁNDEZ RETAMAR /7
Writing à la carte EDUARDO HERAS LEÓN /11
Defense statement by Antonio Guerrero Rodríguez /18
Five years after our court statements /26
The forest of flags EDEL MORALES /31
Anonymous sound FRANCISCO LÓPEZ SACHA /35
Antonio CINTIO VITIER /39
My teacher, my love MARTA ROJAS /51
Defense statement by Fernando González Llort /56
Five years after our court statements /68
So far and yet so near a message to the Five MIGUEL BARNET /75
Certitude LAIDI FERNÁNDEZ DE JUAN /78
Fernando CINTIO VITIER /83
A different morning for Ramón MARILYN BOBES /95
Defense statement by Ramón Labañino Salazar /104
Five years after our court statements /112
Stars in the number PABLO ARMANDO FERNÁNDEZ /114
Leonardo's bicycle revisited MIGUEL MEJIDES /118
Ramón CINTIO VITIER /122
Two birds, one song NANCY MOREJÓN /133
Defense statement by René González Sehwerert /140

Five years after our court statements /148
Final sentence JESÚS ORTA RUIZ /151
The hole ALBERTO GUERRA NARANJO /153
René CINTIO VITIER /157
The 70-degree right angle DANIEL CHAVARRÍA /169
Defense statement by Gerardo Hernández Nordelo /176
Five years after our court statements /183
Warning CÉSAR LÓPEZ /186
The World, Middle Ages MYLENE FERNÁNDEZ PINTADO /189
Gerardo CINTIO VITIER /195
Some key questions about the Cuban Five LEONARD WEINGLASS /207
The Five will be back LISANDRO OTERO /215
Epilogue RICARDO ALARCÓN DE QUESADA /221
The sentences /225
The authors /227

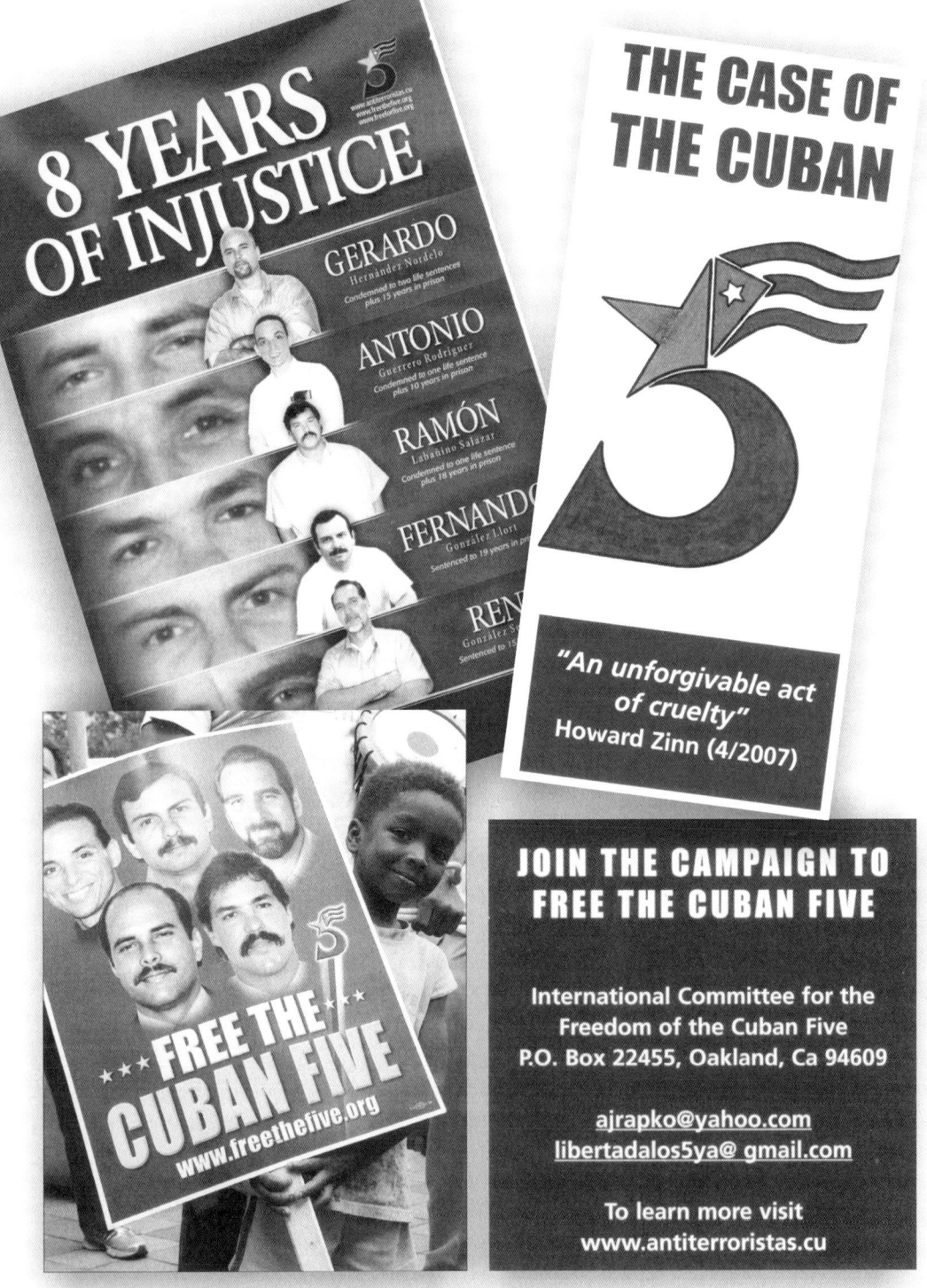